"Paul Mallard's contentior
too focused on the present
about heaven. With ch
explains clearly, faithfully a
teaches about heaven and the new creation, answering the many questions we naturally have about our life after death. He clears away common misunderstandings and gives the reader a compelling and attractive vision of life with Christ and his people. Those who read this book will be stirred to a more confident hope, deeper longing to be with Christ, and comforted to face the struggles of living in this present age."

John Stevens, National Director, FIEC

"In this winsome, clear, and compassionate book, Pastor Mallard offers a beautiful and thorough exposition of the Bible's insights on heaven. Whether you're shepherding a loved one through the end of life, facing the shadowy valley yourself, or seeking to transform your outlook with the truths of Scripture, *Heaven* offers theological riches that will comfort you, instill you with hope, and point you to the One who is making all things new."

Kathryn Butler, MD, author of *Between Life and Death* and *Glimmers of Grace*

"Soaked in Scripture and laced with a blend of glorious theology and the practical wisdom and winsomeness that accompanies everything Paul writes and teaches, *Heaven* is a book that answers many of our questions and inspires our souls with a Christ intoxicated longing. I thoroughly recommend it."

Jeremy McQuoid, Teaching Pastor at Deeside Christian Fellowship

HE
AV
EN

PAUL MALLARD

HEAVEN

LIVING WITH ETERNITY IN VIEW

Evangelical Press

First published in Great Britain in 2025

British Library Cataloguing in Publication Data
A record for this book is available from the British Library

ISBN: 978-1-78397-489-4

Designed by Pete Barnsley (CreativeHoot.com)

Printed in the UK

Evangelical Press, an imprint of 10Publishing
Unit C, Tomlinson Road, Leyland, PR25 2DY, England

info@10ofthose.com
www.10ofthose.com

1 3 5 7 10 8 6 4 2

For Julie

After that, we who are still alive and are left will be caught up together with them in the clouds to meet the Lord in the air. And so we will be with the Lord for ever.

Therefore encourage one another with these words.

CONTENTS

PART 1

SO MANY QUESTIONS

My dad was a big bloke.

After the war he married my mum and worked in a grocer's shop in Birmingham. Back in the forties the shopkeeper cut the bacon on a bacon slicer. I remember the tapestry of scars on his hands where he had come too close to the rotating blade.

He was a great dad and my childhood was very happy. He wasn't a Christian but when I was converted at eleven, he and my mum were fully supportive.

When he was fifty he came to visit me for the weekend at college. We talked about my faith and I gave him a daily devotional to read. A couple of days later I got a letter from him. I have it in front of me now. Dad wrote:

> "I was up at 6:00 this morning so I had time to read a passage from *Every Day With Jesus* regarding the meaning of the cross. I shall continue to read one each morning. I also prayed and invited God into my heart. I was very impressed with the passage Revelation 3:20, 'Behold I stand at the door and knock. If any man hear my voice and open I will come into him and I will sup with him and he with me.' I'm glad we talked together this weekend Paul, I begin to realize the joy you must derive from your Christian life."

It was no flash in the pan. Dad became a disciple of Christ. He was baptized and became a deacon in the church where my wife Edrie and I were converted. He loved Jesus, devoured the Bible and had a simple and obvious joy.

At the age of sixty they discovered he had inoperable cancer. He was given six months. He lasted nine.

My dad was a big bloke, but the cancer diminished him. He seemed to shrink physically. But his spirit and his faith were strong. Along with my mum and sister, I nursed my dad during the last three days of his life. He still had big hands covered with tiny scars. I held his hands and we talked about heaven.

"Tell me about it. Most of all tell me about Jesus. I can't wait to see him," he said.

As we talked together I think we both felt God's presence with us in the valley of the shadow of death. We had a glimpse of glory.

My dad died at 10:15 in the morning on 31 July 1985. It was the day before his sixty-first birthday.

But was he right? Was he going to see Jesus? Is heaven real? Does it exist at this very moment in time? Would he even be conscious of anything?

We buried my dad, with words about the sure and certain hope of the resurrection of the dead.

But what does that mean? Can we have any certainty or is it just wishful thinking? Is hope the worthless crutch on which feeble people who cannot face reality rest their weight?

And if there is such a place as heaven, what will it be like? Where will it be? Who will be there? Will we know each other? What will we do?

We all have questions about heaven. God does not tell us everything we might want to know, but he tells us everything we need to know. In this first section I will explore some fundamental questions about the nature of the home Jesus is preparing for us.

By the end of this book I hope to have answered many of your questions. But more than that, my sincere desire is that a glimpse of glory will change your life.

CHAPTER 1

WHERE IS YOUR HEART?

I was fourteen when I read *Tortured for Christ* by Richard Wurmbrand.

Wurmbrand was a Romanian pastor during the dark days when the Communist Party persecuted the church. He was imprisoned for fourteen years for the crime of preaching Christ. He was regularly tortured. For the rest of his life he bore the scars.

Years after reading the book, I had the privilege of listening to him speak. I will never forget what he said:

> "Some nights I would sit in my cell feeling pain in every part of my body. I was cold and hungry and exhausted. And yet I would sing songs of joy. My captors could take away my possessions and my comforts. They could take away my family and my freedom. They could take away my dignity and my health. They could even take away my life. But what they could not take from me was the

> grip of the nail pierced hands of my Saviour. They could not take my Jesus from me."

The room fell silent as he opened his heart. I sat there stunned by the impact of his words.

Why did the book and the talk make such a big impact on me? Because they made me realize that this world is temporary. God richly blesses us with myriads of gifts which he wants us to enjoy, but in the end all of them are fleeting. Only those things which are eternal will last. And even when we have lost everything else, if we are Christians, we can never lose Jesus. He is our inheritance. In fact, at the heart of heaven is this glorious hope:

> "They will see his face, and his name will be on their foreheads. There will be no more night. They will not need the light of a lamp or the light of the sun, for the Lord God will give them light. And they will reign for ever and ever." (Rev 22:4–5)

Glimpsing this glory will change everything. The purpose of this book is to help us to do just that. And such a glimpse will transform us, so that like Richard Wurmbrand, we will be able to sing songs of joy in the darkest moments of our lives.

Half an hour a day

When my dad died I began a quest to find out as much about heaven as I could. Of course I started with the

Bible but then I began to read what people had written on the subject. Some of it was amazingly fanciful or just downright misleading. But amongst the dross I found some gems. And shining brightest was *The Saints' Everlasting Rest* by the seventeenth-century pastor Richard Baxter.

Baxter served as a pastor in the small town of Kidderminster in the English Midlands. He lived during a turbulent period of history and witnessed civil war, the execution of a king, the birth and death of a republic and the restoration of the monarchy. It was a particularly tempestuous time for believers. Baxter's faithfulness to the gospel led to his ejection from his church, opposition, persecution and imprisonment. On top of this, from an early age he suffered from a whole range of ailments, including kidney stones, chronic pain, tuberculosis and bouts of depression.

His suffering drove him to think about heaven. Baxter challenges us to live our lives in the light of this glorious hope:

> "Take your hearts once again and lead them by the hand. Bring it to the top of the highest mountain. Show it the Kingdom of Christ and the glory of it. Say to your heart, 'All this will your Lord bestow on you … this is your inheritance! This crown is yours. These pleasures are yours. This company is yours. This beauty's place is yours. All things are yours because you are Christ's and Christ is yours.'"[1]

And Baxter practised what he preached. He tells us that from the age of thirty he decided to spend at least half an hour every day thinking about heaven. He lived into his seventies, which means he spent the next forty years meditating daily on heaven!

Was Baxter a fanatic? No! In the New Testament heaven is the climax of the "3 Rs" which are the blueprint for God's future purposes – the Return of Christ; the Resurrection; and the Restoration of all things. It is the eternal destiny of all God's people. Throughout the New Testament, heaven is constantly set before us as a motive for holy living and faithful service and confident suffering.

And yet it seems to be the last thing we think about. When was the last time you meditated on heaven? When was the last time you heard a sermon or read a book or had a conversation about heaven?

It seems we no longer think or talk or prepare for heaven as much as people of previous generations. It is largely absent from many of our hymns and sermons and prayers. How do we explain this eclipse of heaven in contemporary Christianity?

The eclipse of heaven

There may well be a whole series of complicated reasons for this loss of emphasis. In the West many of us have such a comfortable existence that, although heaven seems to be a great idea, we are quite happy with our earthly lot and reluctant to let it go. In the past, when life was shorter and more uncertain, people found their focus drawn to eternal things. Cemeteries were filled with children who had died in infancy sadly underlining the brevity of life and the closeness of eternity.

It may be controversial to say this, but after four decades as a pastor I cannot help but notice that in general the church is too focused on the present. Often we are staring at our feet when we should be fixing our eyes on our ultimate destination. The church faces many challenges in the future. It is really important that we have a solid grasp of where we are going.

Then of course there comes the common charge that people who are "heavenly minded are no earthly good". C.S. Lewis refuted this many years ago:

> "If you read history you will find that the Christians who did the most for the present world are just the ones that thought the most of the next. The apostles themselves, who set afoot the conversion of the Roman Empire, the great men who built up the Middle Ages, the English Evangelicals who abolished the Slave Trade, all left their mark on Earth, precisely because their minds were occupied with Heaven. It is since Christians have largely ceased to think of the other world that they have become so ineffective in this. Think about Heaven and you'll get the earth 'thrown in': aim at earth and you'll get neither."[2]

Out of love for our neighbours we should be fully engaged in this world, but there is a very real sense that it is not our home – not, at least, until God has re-created it. Peter reminds his hearers that they are exiles scattered throughout the Roman Empire (1 Pet 1:1) who are to set their "hope on the grace to be brought to you when Jesus Christ is revealed at his coming" (1 Pet 1:13). He goes on to instruct them:

> "Dear friends, I urge you, as foreigners and exiles, to abstain from sinful desires, which wage war against your soul. Live such good lives among the pagans that, though they accuse you of doing wrong, they may see your good deeds and glorify God on the day he visits us." (1 Pet 2:11–12)

Notice that they are not to opt out of engaging with their pagan neighbours, but they are to recognize that they do not belong here. In the final analysis, we do not need to make a choice between engaging with this world and longing for the heavenly hope of a new creation.

Yet the charge persists and still finds traction.

But maybe the principal reason for our reluctance to think about heaven is that it is often presented as such a totally unappetizing prospect. It is portrayed as an other-worldly existence somewhere off in space with no connection to the present creation. In the popular imagination the afterlife is a place of eternal disembodied hymn singing.

As we shall see this is not what the Bible teaches. According to Scripture the hope of the Bible is for a new creation which will involve the total transformation of this present creation. In other words our hope is not way off in space, but right here. In a world washed clean we will worship and serve God and enjoy him forever.

The aim of this book is to explore what the Bible teaches about the nature of our heavenly life. My hope and prayer is that lifting our eyes to heaven will create a better and more rounded perspective on our lives now. How can I live the most fruitful Christian life today? Part of the answer is to be aware of a better life to come. Gazing at glory will strengthen our walk of faith and prepare us for trouble and trial.

Paul reminds us that "no eye has seen … no ear has heard, and … no human mind has conceived the things God has prepared for those who love him", so we should approach with caution. However, Paul goes on to assure us that "these are the things God has revealed to us by his Spirit" (1 Cor 2:9–10).

We have a joyful duty to explore what God has revealed.

Many reasons

I hope that I have already persuaded you that Christians should think more about heaven than we currently do, but if I haven't, let me give you four more reasons.

1. It is commanded

Paul instructs the Christians in Colossae:

> "Since, then, you have been raised with Christ, set your hearts on things above, where Christ is, seated at the right hand of God. Set your minds on things above, not on earthly things. For you died, and your life is now hidden with Christ in God. When Christ, who is your life, appears, then you also will appear with him in glory." (Col 3:1–4)

We will return to these words towards the end of the book. For the moment just notice that Paul justifies his command with the reminder that their lives are intimately connected with the life of Christ. Jesus is in heaven – why wouldn't you want to fix your gaze there?

In the verses that follow these glorious commands, Paul also blows out of the water the false idea that being heavenly minded makes us uninterested in this world. Focusing on heaven will affect our lifestyles, marriages, parenting and attitude to work (Col 3:5–25).

2. It means that we will be with Jesus

The central attraction of heaven is the presence of Jesus. Seeing dismay and fear in the faces of his disciples just a few hours before he went to the cross, Jesus spoke words of comfort. He was going to the cross in order to prepare a place for them in heaven so that they could be with him forever:

> "Do not let your hearts be troubled. You believe in God; believe also in me. My Father's house has many rooms;

> if that were not so, would I have told you that I am going there to prepare a place for you? And if I go and prepare a place for you, I will come back and take you to be with me that you also may be where I am." (John 14:1–3)

The Bridegroom's departure is not a divorce, just a temporary separation.

The highest aspiration we can have and the one which should transform us now is the longing to be with our Saviour. Jesus is the treasure secured in heaven and waiting to welcome us.

3. It is wise

Psalm 90, the Psalm of Moses, is a meditation on the contrast between the holiness and eternal nature of God and the sinfulness and the brevity of human life. Moses writes against the background of the deaths of a whole generation of the people in the wilderness:

> "Lord, you have been our dwelling place
> throughout all generations.
> Before the mountains were born
> or you brought forth the whole world,
> from everlasting to everlasting you are God.
>
> You turn people back to dust,
> saying, 'Return to dust, you mortals.'
> … you sweep people away in the sleep of death –
> they are like the new grass of the morning:

> In the morning it springs up new,
>   but by evening it is dry and withered."
> (Psalm 90:1–3, 5–6)

How should we respond? Verse 12 tells us: "Teach us to number our days, that we may gain a heart of wisdom." To look soberly at the brevity of life and the vastness of eternity is to be heavenly minded, and to be heavenly minded is to be wise.

4. It helps us endure with courage

The Christian life is not easy. We live in a war zone grappling against a violent and malicious opponent. How do we endure? How do we keep going when we feel like giving up?

The letter to the Hebrews is written to people who face serious opposition. To encourage them the author reminds them that although it may be difficult to go forward, it is impossible to go back! He reminds them of the example of previous generations of believers. They endured all sorts of things because their eyes were on the final goal – a goal that was ultimately beyond this world, "whose architect and builder is God" (Heb 11:10).

And of course the supreme example of endurance is the Lord Jesus himself:

> "... let us run with perseverance the race marked out for us, fixing our eyes on Jesus, the pioneer and perfecter of faith. For the joy set before him he endured the cross,

> scorning its shame, and sat down at the right hand of the throne of God. Consider him who endured such opposition from sinners, so that you will not grow weary and lose heart." (Heb 12:1–3)

In Christ, God did not walk away from human need. He rolled up his sleeves and got his hands dirty. To save us he went further and actually got his hands bloody. At the same time in the midst of the direst trials he endured with joy because his eye was on the prize.

To be heavenly minded is to glimpse glory, then fix our eyes on the prize and keep going.

CHAPTER 2

WHERE IS YOUR HOPE?

Florence Chadwick was an exceptional woman.

Born in San Diego, California, on 9 November 1918, Florence grew up near the beach and began competitive swimming at the age of six. In the early 1950s she became the first woman to swim the English channel in both directions. In 1952 she took on an even more demanding challenge.

Twenty-six miles off the coast of California lies the beautiful Santa Catalina Island. On 4 July Florence attempted to become the first woman to swim from the island to the mainland. She was accompanied by a small flotilla of boats. Some of the sailors carried rifles to drive off sharks! The weather was cold for the season and as she began there was the hint of fog. Soon the hint became a reality and the boats accompanying Florence had to work hard to keep her in their sights. Then the waters became choppier and the wind picked up.

For fifteen hours and fifty-five minutes Florence laboured on. During the last hour it was only courage and determination that kept her going. In the end even that failed. From one of the boats her mother assured her that she was almost home, but Florence was physically and emotionally exhausted and begged to be taken on board.

She discovered that she had less than a mile to swim to complete the challenge.

Speaking to the press the next day she described her experience in the water and then said: "All I could see was the fog … I think if I could have seen the shore, I would have made it."[1]

Life is difficult. Our circumstances vary hugely and in times of ease we may be complacent and have little thought of heaven. But this is an illusion. The only qualification for suffering is to live long enough. No one is immune. We have to battle through pain and peril, doubt and depression, trial and trouble. We lose our health or our financial security or our loved ones. On top of that we are surrounded with a world full of pain. There are times when it all feels overwhelming and we would love to be hauled out of adversity into the warm security of a pain-free existence.

It is in these situations that we need to see the shore.

Seeing the shore is what the Bible calls hope.

An anchor for the soul

The recipients of the letter to the Hebrews were facing the seas of adverse circumstances. The author of the letter picks up this metaphor and encourages them to live in hope. Hope is like an anchor which keeps us secure:

> "We have this hope as an anchor for the soul, firm and secure. It enters the inner sanctuary behind the curtain, where our forerunner, Jesus, has entered on our behalf." (Heb 6:19–20)

Like an anchor, hope gives us confidence and security. It gives stability to life as it latches onto the certainty of the promises of God. This hope, you will notice, is focused on Jesus, our great High Priest. He is the author and finisher of our faith (Heb 12:2) who has ascended to heaven (Heb 4:14) where he "sat down at the right hand of the throne of the Majesty in heaven" (Heb 8:1). He is "holy, blameless, pure, set apart from sinners, exalted above the heavens" (Heb 7:26). He has already reached the shore of heaven and he assures us that we will safely arrive. It is as we contemplate this that our hopes are nourished.

The world around us thinks of hope as vague wishful thinking. "I hope it will happen. I'll keep my fingers crossed. But don't hold your breath!" In the Bible hope is the exact opposite of this. Hope in Scripture is shorthand for unconditional certainty. My hope is not nebulous and tenuous, it is confident and guaranteed. This is because gaining heaven does not depend on me and my endurance but upon God and his faithfulness.

And hope is vital to human flourishing. Unlike other creatures we have an active imagination and we are future orientated. We need to look forward with an assurance that things will somehow get better. To lose hope is to lose direction and to be plunged into despair. On the gates of hell the Italian poet Dante sees the inscription, "ABANDON EVERY HOPE, [YOU] WHO ENTER HERE".[2] To live without hope is to cease to thrive as a human being.

Bearing that in mind, recall how Paul describes people in the world who live without Christ:

> "... remember that at that time you were separate from Christ, excluded from citizenship in Israel and foreigners to the covenants of the promise, without hope and without God in the world." (Eph 2:12)

People we meet every day may appear to have everything together and to be living well ordered and happy lives, but they are without God and without hope. Any hope for the future and for eternity which is not based on God and his promises is groundless and will prove to be an illusion when we face the judgement of God on the last day.

More loved than we ever dared hope

In the Bible faith, hope and love are often associated as a glorious triumvirate. We know that the greatest is love (1 Cor 13:13) and we are convicted that faith is necessary if we are to please God (Heb 11:6), but sometimes hope is neglected. It feels a bit like a poor relation. However this is not how the Bible sees it. In the Bible hope is sometimes seen as the spring from which other virtues flow. Listen to Paul's words to the Colossians:

> "We always thank God, the Father of our Lord Jesus Christ, when we pray for you, because we have heard of your faith in Christ Jesus and of the love you have for all God's people – the faith and love that spring from the hope stored up for you in heaven and about which you have already heard in the true message of the gospel ..." (Col 1:3–5)

The gospel message which they heard was the "hope stored up for you in heaven". This produced faith in Christ and love for God's people.

It is difficult to overestimate the importance of hope in the letters of Paul. He tells the Ephesians:

> "I pray that the eyes of your heart may be enlightened in order that you may know the hope to which he has called you, the riches of his glorious inheritance in his holy people ..." (Eph 1:18)

This hope is nothing less than "Christ in you, the hope of glory" (Col 1:27) and is like a helmet protecting our heads and enabling us to think straight (Eph 6:17). We are those who:

> "... wait for the blessed hope – the appearing of the glory of our great God and Saviour, Jesus Christ, who

gave himself for us to redeem us from all wickedness and to purify for himself a people that are his very own, eager to do what is good." (Titus 2:13–14)

Christ's love and grace surpasses all our wildest dreams and expectations. As Timothy Keller says, despite our sin and flaws, "we are more loved and accepted in Jesus Christ than we ever dared hope".[3] His love secures our place in heaven and the contemplation of this changes everything. At this moment in time you may feel that the waters are choppy, that the wind is against you and that the fog is impenetrable. Keep your eyes on the shore. Jesus is your anchor and your eternal reward.

Keep going!

A solid foundation

To grasp this hope more firmly we will turn from Paul to Peter who writes his first letter to a group of Christians who are "exiles", scattered in dozens of towns and cities across the Roman Province of Asia Minor – modern-day Turkey (1 Pet 1:1). Although they reside there, they will never quite belong.

As believers they are to live out the implications of the fact their citizenship is in heaven. Peter rejoices because they are people of a living hope, a hope that animates and transforms:

"Praise be to the God and Father of our Lord Jesus Christ! In his great mercy he has given us new birth into

> a living hope through the resurrection of Jesus Christ from the dead, and into an inheritance that can never perish, spoil or fade. This inheritance is kept in heaven for you, who through faith are shielded by God's power until the coming of the salvation that is ready to be revealed in the last time." (1 Pet 1:3–5)

This hope is an excited and confident expectation of fullness of life in the future. But what are the grounds for this hope? How can sinful people like us ever have a hope of a heaven which is utterly holy and sin-free?

Peter bases this hope on three solid foundations.

Firstly we can have a heavenly hope because of the "great mercy" of our God and Father. We might translate it as the "abundant mercy" or the "much mercy". A little mercy will not suffice. As rebels we deserve God's wrath – instead we have received his unearned and undeserved mercy. He has tender-hearted, loving compassion for those who are helpless and hopeless.

When I started in ministry I was mentored by an elderly pastor named Ebenezer Knight. He was still preaching into his seventies. He had lived an exemplary Christian life and served God faithfully to the end. During my last meeting with Eb we talked about heaven. Without a hint of false modesty he solemnly confessed: "I will be looking to mercy. I found mercy many years ago. Now as I come to the end I have nowhere else to go. I will be looking to mercy."

But we should remember that as free as mercy is to us, it is incredibly costly to God. The cost of God's mercy and of our hope is "the precious blood of Christ, a lamb without blemish or defect" (1 Pet 1:19).

The second foundation of our hope is the gift of new birth. We have been given new life by the Holy Spirit – indeed we have begun to experience something of the life of heaven now. The term echoes Jesus' words to Nicodemus: "Very truly I tell you, no one can see the kingdom of God unless they are born again" (John 3:3).

The phrase may be translated "born from above". Like mercy we don't earn or achieve this rebirth. God takes the initiative. He reaches down to dead people and grants them life where before there was only spiritual death. Anyone in Christ is a new creation – "the old has gone, the new is here!" (2 Cor 5:17). It is personal, supernatural and radical.

And it is vital. We will never be ready for the life of heaven unless God breathes new life into our souls now. The phrase "born-again Christian" has been widely misused and is often drained of any biblical meaning. However when understood rightly, it is an accurate description of those who are true believers and who therefore share the Christian hope.

The third and final foundation for our hope is an objective and non-negotiable fact of history. Hope comes to us through "the resurrection of Jesus Christ from the dead" (1 Pet 1:3). Jesus really died, he really rose and it really matters. It really matters because he is "the firstfruits of those who have fallen asleep" (1 Cor 15:20). The resurrection of Jesus proves that death will not have the last word. It could not hold him (Acts 2:24). We have a living hope because Jesus is a living Saviour.

For many years merchants and explorers attempted to find a route from Europe to India around the southern tip of Africa. It proved elusive because the waters of the cape were so treacherous. In 1488 Bartolomeu Dias was the first to round the cape. He was followed by the Portuguese explorer Vasco da Gama in 1498 who returned with rich merchandise from the Indies. The "Cape of Storms" became the "Cape of Good Hope".

Jesus passed through death, the king of terrors, and returned. Death is still an enemy, but it is no longer the ogre it once was. For believers the resurrection of Jesus has given us a good and living hope.

A glorious inheritance

Peter goes on to describe the contents of the hope which God's people will enjoy. In doing this he uses the carefully chosen word "inheritance". In the Old Testament the people of Israel were to obtain an earthly inheritance in the Promised Land (Deut 2:12; 12:9; Josh 11:23). They were not yet in the land when God promised it to them but the promise was so sure that they could think of it as already belonging to them. It was an unearned gift of grace. Christians have been given mercy and new birth so that we can obtain an inheritance, not in the land of Canaan, but in the heavenly kingdom.

To describe this kingdom Peter uses a series of negatives. This is often the case when Bible writers want to describe the heavenly country. They want to contrast it with our present experience.

Our inheritance will "never perish, spoil or fade".

It is imperishable. It is not subject to the ravages of time or the devastations of decay. Everything we see, or touch or possess in this world will perish, but not our inheritance. Disease, decay, corrosion and death cannot touch it.

It is undefiled. It is unstained by sin. Even the best and most godly things in this world are polluted by the sin which clings so closely. Every relationship, every church, every act of service is vulnerable to the corruption and defilement which even the finest believer finds lurking in their hearts. One of the great joys of heaven will be the total banishment of evil forever.

It is unfading. It will never cease to satisfy because it will never wane or wilt or wither. It will never grow dim or lose its lustre or its magnificence. The book of Ecclesiastes reminds us that the things we grasp in this world are passing – a mere "chasing after the wind" (Ecc 2:11) – and can never satisfy the deepest longings of our hearts. This is not true of our inheritance.

But I think we can go further. Not all the Israelites had a physical portion of the land as their inheritance. The priests and the tribe of Levi had cities to dwell in but no land to possess. God gave them something better:

> "The LORD said to Aaron, 'You will have no inheritance in their land, nor will you have any share among them; I am your share and your inheritance among the Israelites.'" (Num 18:20)

The Lord himself was to be their inheritance. As we shall see again and again, the central attraction of heaven, the thing that makes heaven really heaven, is the presence of God. It is God who is eternal, unchangeable and imperishable. It is God who is utterly pure, holy and undefiled. It is God whose majesty and beauty never tarnishes or loses its bloom or ceases to eternally satisfy our souls. The enjoyment of heaven is the enjoyment of God.

As believers labouring against treacherous seas isn't it good to see the shore?

A safe landing

But can we, personally, be sure of reaching the shore? Peter addresses this concern with two assertions.

Firstly, our inheritance is kept in heaven for us. God has stored up our inheritance in heaven so that nothing can destroy it. We are among "the church of the firstborn, whose names are written in heaven" (Heb 12:23). This is the source of real and unceasing joy (Luke 10:20). Our inheritance is kept in the safest possible place and reserved for the day we can fully enjoy it.

Secondly, Peter assures them that they will be kept safe. They are those "who through faith are shielded by

God's power until the coming of the salvation that is ready to be revealed in the last time" (1 Pet 1:5). There is a wonderful symmetry here. If you are in the midst of a stormy sea it may be encouraging to know that your treasure is secure on the shore, but what about you if the boat goes down? You need to be sure you are guaranteed a safe landing. And this is the very assurance that he gives us here.

We are shielded until the day we reach the shore. Peter uses a military term meaning to be guarded or carefully watched over. The tense is continuous – you are being permanently guarded – guarded for as long as is necessary. And God is guarding us through our own personal faith, which he strengthens and energizes by his invincible power.

Two months after being pulled out of the sea just off the coast of California, Florence Chadwick made a second attempt at the Catalina swim. The same thick fog set in, but this time she made it. She said that she kept a mental image of the shoreline in her mind while she swam. She later swam the Catalina channel on two additional occasions.

Florence died of leukaemia in San Diego in 1995; her ashes were scattered into the ocean off Point Loma.

In the midst of raging seas and in the face of death itself it is good to remember that we have a positive answer to the questions posed in Priscilla Jane Owen's hymn:

"Will your anchor hold in the floods of death,
when the waters cold chill your latest breath? …
Will your eyes behold through the morning light
the city of gold and the harbour bright?
Will you anchor safe by the heavenly shore,
when life's storms are past for evermore?"[4]

The answer is a resounding "Yes!"

Our hope is eternal in its dimensions. One day the storms will be over and we will reach the harbour bright.

CHAPTER 3

WHAT'S THE BIG PICTURE?

I had been a pastor for a couple of years when I had a very unusual phone call from a local GP: "I'm not a Christian," he said, "but I thought that you could help. I have a patient called Joyce who has learning difficulties. She has fallen into the clutches of the Jehovah's Witnesses. She is desperate to leave but doesn't know how. They won't stop calling on her. Can you help?"

I could and I did! Joyce was housebound so a couple of us made sure we were there at the next visit of the "missionaries". Our presence gave Joyce the support she needed to cut the ties and they never returned.

Joyce asked us if we would visit her again. Over the next few years two ladies from the church visited her every week and taught her to read using the Bible.

It was great to see her excitement: "I've been reading this bit in the Bible Pastor. Did you know that Jesus actually walked on the water!"

"Yes, I think I'd heard that!" I replied.

One day I was met with the usual enthusiasm. "Pastor I've just been reading the last book in the Bible – the revolutions of John."

"Great Joyce. Did you understand it?"

"Not much. But I loved the last bit. In the end Jesus will come back and he will put everything right."

Shortly after that Joyce came to faith and I had the joy of baptizing her.

Joyce was spot on in her description – the Revelation of John is revolutionary! It is God's last word to mankind and it's all about heaven.

The common notion is that Revelation is obscure and incomprehensible. I do not agree! It's not some kind of fiendish sudoku. It's God's picture book. There are plenty of difficult passages to wrestle with, but Joyce had grasped the thrust of the book. Written to Christians who are being crushed by persecution and mesmerized by false teachers, Jesus reveals that there are evil forces in the world that will always oppose God and seek to destroy his people. But Jesus is alive, he reigns from heaven and he will return in glory to put everything right.

To encourage these suffering Christians, Jesus draws back the curtain of time and uncovers the ultimate destiny of our world. In this chapter, we will introduce the main themes of Revelation's glorious climactic vision recorded in 21:1–22:6.

The vision can be divided into three sections:

A renewed cosmos

John begins this final section of Revelation with the broadest possible vista as he describes a whole new creation:

> "Then I saw 'a new heaven and a new earth,' for the first heaven and the first earth had passed away, and there was no longer any sea." (Rev 21:1)

John deliberately echoes the first words of the Bible as he describes the new heaven and earth. Just as God made everything out of nothing by the power of his word, so now he is the sole architect of all things in the new creation. Just like a wonderful piece of art which has been defaced by ugly graffiti, creation today is beautiful but marred. We have never seen an uncursed tree or an uncursed mountain. The renewed creation will be washed clean and made perfect.

In biblical symbolism the sea is often a picture of disorder, rebellion and chaos. God subdued the chaos of the waters (Exod 14) and Jesus proves his deity by subduing the sea (Matt 14:22–33). The absence of the seas is therefore probably symbolic, giving us a foretaste of an ordered and peaceful new creation.

As John marvels over this new creation, a city descends:

> "I saw the Holy City, the new Jerusalem, coming down out of heaven from God, prepared as a bride beautifully dressed for her husband." (Rev 21:2)

Old Testament saints were looking for a city created by God (Heb 11:10). It has finally arrived. To mix the metaphor, this long-awaited city is like a bride on her wedding day. John has already described the marriage supper of the Lamb and elsewhere we see the bride is none other than the church (Eph 5:25–33). So is this city a location or is it the church? My view is both. In this bride-gown-wearing city, we have a wonderful picture of the church and of her final dwelling place.

The most important thing to notice is the city's origin. Here is a city not built by human hands or the result of strenuous human effort. It comes down from heaven. God brings it into existence – his new creation by water and the word. This city is the Christian's ultimate home (Phil 3:20).

For the first time John hears a voice coming from the throne. It alerts him to the defining characteristic of the new creation. This city is nothing less than the home of God:

> "Look! God's dwelling place is now among the people, and he will dwell with them. They will be his people, and God himself will be with them and be their God." (Rev 21:3)

In the Old Testament God came to dwell amongst his people in a tabernacle (Exod 40:34–35) and a temple (2 Chron 7:1–3). But this was provisional and temporary. Sin drove his glory from the temple (Ezek 10). But John sees the permanent dwelling place of God amongst men and women in the new creation. The delights of eternity focus on the intimacy of this relationship.

And in an amazingly intimate picture of compassion, the first thing God does for his people is to stoop down and wipe away all tears:

> "'He will wipe every tear from their eyes. There will be no more death' or mourning or crying or pain, for the old order of things has passed away." (Rev 21:4)

This world is a vale of tears – we weep for our own sorrows and for the sorrows of others. Death touches all of us. To love and lose is to suffer. But this is "the old order of things". It will not last into the new creation. Every stain of sin; every scar of wrong; every trace of death will be removed forever.

There will be no more hospitals or funerals; no broken homes or broken hearts; no wheelchairs or spectacles; no diabetes or cancer or heart disease or Alzheimer's; no mental illness or depression; no disease, disorder, disaster or death. We live in the middle of the book where all these painful things hold temporary sway. It is almost impossible to imagine a world without them. But none of the things described in verse 4 were present in Eden in the first two chapters of the Bible. In the last two chapters of the Bible they are again absent and will be forever.

All this sounds wonderful; almost too good to be true. The one on the throne encourages John to write down what he has seen (Rev 21:5) and gives a personal assurance that the reader can rely totally on his words (Rev 21:6–7). He is the one who stands at the beginning and end of all things – the Alpha and the Omega. There is a battle all the way to heaven, but those who persevere will be satisfied with the free gift of the water of life and will inherit what God has promised.

But there is a sting in the tail.

If there is a heaven to win there is also a hell to avoid (Rev 21:8). Those who live lives in deliberate rebellion will experience the second death. If physical death involves the separation of the body and the soul, then the second death refers to the eternal separation of the entire person from the life of God. This verse describes the lifestyle of those who rebel against God. They are those whose names are not written in the book of life (Rev 20:15). Personal faith in Christ is the only way in which we can enjoy the blessings of the new creation.

A radiant city

John now describes the glory of the city of God. The images in Revelation 21:9–27 are supposed to take our breath away. We don't have to take them literally to be amazed at the magnificence of the overall picture they provide of both the church and its ultimate location. John Newton captured this in the words of a great hymn:

> "Glorious things of thee are spoken,
> Zion, city of our God!

He, whose Word cannot be broken,
formed thee for His own abode;
On the Rock of Ages founded,
what can shake thy sure repose?
With salvation's walls surrounded,
thou may'st smile at all thy foes."[1]

An angel acts as John's tour guide as he explores this city. This expert guide sweeps John through the city, explaining its origin, showing John its structure and dimensions, and allowing John to admire its beauty, glory and purity.

We are told again that the city is the bride of the Lamb – confirming that this is a picture of the church. The city shines with precious stones, symbolizing the glory of God. It comes down from heaven. At the tower of Babel people joined together to create a monument to their own glory. The new Jerusalem is God's gift, not man's achievement. This should not lead to disengagement from the world, but it should prompt us to long for the return of Christ.

Next John takes in the walls which reveal the safety and security of the city (Rev 21:12–14). However, the gates are never shut (Rev 21:25), because all enemies have been eliminated! The architecture represents the presence of both Old and New Testament saints. The twelve gates with the names of the twelve tribes represent all God's people in the Old Testament. The twelve foundations with the names of the twelve apostles point to all God's people in the New Testament and Christian era. All the saints of both testaments and the whole of history have a home here.

John's tour guide has a measuring rod and the city covers an impressive area: 12,000 stadia – that's 14,000 miles – in every direction (Rev 21:15–17). This is further than the distance between London and Wellington, New Zealand. It is massive – bigger than the Roman Empire. The empires of this earth will perish, but God's city will last forever.

The size also indicates the multitude of its inhabitants – a number that no one can count (Rev 7:9). And, significantly, it forms a perfect cube. The only other cube in the Bible is the Holy of Holies in the temple (2 Chron 3:8). The whole city is God's Holy of Holies and here he will dwell with us forever.

John describes the beauty of the walls and street and gates of the city (Rev 21:18–21). Jewels, pearls and gold are symbolic of its magnificence. Perhaps they are to remind us of the precious gems carried on the breastplate of the High Priest (Exod 28:17–20). The High Priest was able to enter God's immediate presence. In the new creation we will also experience a new intimacy.

Amongst all the beauty, what is the ultimate glory of the city? It is that God dwells at its centre (Rev 21:22–26). There is no temple building because God is its temple. His presence is the constant blessing bestowed on his people for eternity. Its splendour is augmented by the fact that the glory of the nations will be brought into it. None of the treasures forged by the nations during their long history will be lost. Think of the finest art and the most magnificent music and the glories of human achievement. They will all be there.

A restored paradise

Gardens abound in Scripture. Our first parents enjoyed the delights of the garden of Eden (Gen 2). Exiled from the presence of God and from the joys of the garden they became wanderers in the earth, longing for home.

In another garden the Son of God bowed his head to his Father's will (Mark 14:32–42). He then went into the darkness and exile of Calvary where he bore the punishment for our sins.

Three days later, in a garden tomb, death was defeated and life and immortality were brought to light. And so the way back into God's presence has been won. It is fitting therefore that the final picture John sees is of a garden. This garden is one of delight – paradise restored. It is reminiscent of Eden with its trees (Gen 2:9; Rev 22:1–2) and rivers (Gen 2:10–14; Rev 22:1). However it is better than Eden. A snake had access to the first garden and tempted the first Adam. In the final garden Satan has been neutralized by the last Adam. Because of the work of Christ, the snake is banished and we will live there forever. There is no exit sign in this garden!

What is life like in this garden?

Abundant life

John sees the river of the water of life (Rev 22:1–2) which symbolizes the eternal life which Christ offers. Think of his words to the woman at the well:

> "Everyone who drinks this water will be thirsty again, but whoever drinks the water I give them will never thirst. Indeed, the water I give them will become in them a spring of water welling up to eternal life." (John 4:13–14)

Eternal life is to know the only true God and Jesus Christ whom he sent (John 17:3). We taste this deep and refreshing water now but in the future we will taste life in an even greater fullness. Notice in Revelation 22:1 that the water flows from the throne of God and the Lamb. This is not a throne of judgement, but of grace and abundant blessing. God is the source of our life.

This is further symbolized by the tree of life (cf Gen 2:9) bearing twelve crops of fruit. Its yield is perpetual, abundant and therapeutic. Adam and Eve were forbidden to eat of the tree because of their sin (Gen 3:22–23). Death is the common experience of the human race. In the new creation health and wellness are the perpetual benediction of all God's people.

Constant activity

In Revelation 22:3–5, the presence of God is again affirmed, and the picture is one of constant activity. His servants serve him and reign with him. These two verbs perfectly capture our relationship with God. On the one hand we are happy servants of a glorious Master. We belong to our Master and delight to do his will. On the other hand we are kings and priests (1 Pet 2:9) and we will reign with Christ forever (Rev 5:9–10). Jesus captured both aspects when he spoke about his faithful servants ruling over cities (Luke 19:12–26).

It is not entirely clear what this will look like, but we will be real people exercising real dominion over a real world made new by God's grace and power. We do know that the task given to Adam will be renewed in the last Adam and his people. As with so many truths about heaven we can only look forward with glad anticipation and growing wonder that God's grace turns rebels into rulers.

In heaven there is both rest and activity. We will find rest from doubts and fears, from conflict and failure and from pain and death. And with the curse removed we will also enjoy the satisfaction of work well done and activity without drudgery.

Intimate communion

There is much to excite us about eternity, but the greatest attraction of heaven is not the absence of pain or the presence of the people we love. The highest bliss and the deepest delight is encapsulated in these words: "They will see his face, and his name will be on their foreheads" (Rev 22:4).

Adam and Eve walked with God in the cool of the day. That close companionship was lost when they sinned. At the present time we cannot see God and survive the encounter (Exod 33:20). But in heaven we will see him face to face. And we are marked with his name on our foreheads, indicating intimacy, security and identity.

The night with its fears and dangers is gone forever. Just as there is no need for a temple because God is the temple, so now there is no need for human lamps or lights. Jesus is the water of life which refreshes the soul. He is also light in the darkness:

> "I am the light of the world. Whoever follows me will never walk in darkness but will have the light of life." (John 8:12)

We will walk in the light of his smile for eternity.

Here then is God's big picture of heaven. We are not meant to get lost in the details. Instead our hearts are to yearn for this and as we yearn we pray:

> "O Lord, support us all the day long
> til the shadows lengthen
> and the evening comes
> and the busy world is hushed
> and the fever of life is over
> and our work is done.

Then in your mercy
grant us a safe lodging
a holy rest
and peace at the last."[2]

CHAPTER 4

WHAT ABOUT ...?

When I retired from full time pastoral ministry my wife and I moved from Bath to Birmingham. We went for the first appointment with our doctor within a few weeks of the move. My wife has a range of serious medical conditions so she had a list of questions she needed to ask. When she had exhausted her list, the doctor asked, "Why on earth did you move from Bath to Birmingham?"

We had a ready-made answer, "Most of our family are nearby and we wanted to be near them."

It's a good answer, but a few days later it dawned on me that there was another reason we wanted to move back. Both my wife and I grew up here. We attended the same infant school and fell in love in the same youth group. We were returning to our roots. We were going home!

As much as we love it here, there is another home that the heart of the Christian aches for. And unlike our earthly homes, we've yet to see this one. In the previous chapter, we surveyed the big picture of what our home in heaven will be like. Glorious as this sweeping look at heaven is, thinking about the specifics may well raise a number of questions in our minds about our future home.

Question one: Where is heaven now?

Is heaven a place or a state of mind? Does it exist at this moment of time or will it come into existence at some future moment either in history or beyond history?

In the Bible the word "heaven" is used in three fundamental ways.[1]

The heavens can refer to the sky or blanket of air which surrounds the earth. We call these the *atmospheric heavens.* Here the birds fly and the clouds take shape. Here we see the rain, lightning and snow. God pours out his material blessings from these heavens:

> "The LORD will open the heavens, the storehouse of his bounty, to send rain on your land in season and to bless all the work of your hands." (Deut 28:12)

When his people rebel, God can close the heavens and withhold his blessing:

> "When the heavens are shut up and there is no rain because your people have sinned against you …" (1 Kings 8:35)

In both of these verses it is clear that the atmospheric heavens belong to God and he rules over them.

The *celestial heavens* lie beyond planet earth and are what we today might refer to as "space". God created and then filled the celestial heavens with the sun, moon and stars. We read:

> "In the heavens God has pitched a tent for the sun."
> (Psalm 19:4)

The heavens declare his glory. Although they are wordless they speak eloquently, clearly, constantly and universally (Psalm 19:1–6). Their vastness is often alluded to as an indication of the power and magnificence of God.

Both the atmospheric and the celestial heavens are real, physical and visible.

But what about the third usage of the word? This speaks of heaven as the place where God lives. We might refer to this heaven as God's throne room. He is "our Father in heaven" (Matt 6:9) and we direct our prayers heavenwards:

> "Look down from heaven, your holy dwelling-place,
> and bless your people Israel …" (Deut 26:15)

Humans are contrasted with God:

> "God is in heaven
> and you are on earth,
> so let your words be few." (Ecc 5:2)

Elsewhere heaven is defined as the place where God has his throne:

> "The LORD is in his holy temple;
> the LORD is on his heavenly throne." (Psalm 11:4)

If we read the symbolism of Revelation 4–5 correctly, we learn heaven exists at the present moment in time. In Revelation 4 John sees a door into heaven and he is invited to enter and observe. Like Isaiah before him (Isa 6:1–6), John glimpses the throne room of heaven. The throne is occupied by one who "had the appearance of jasper and ruby" (Rev 4:3). And angels, living creatures and twenty-four elders ceaselessly worship the one enthroned (Rev 4:4–8).

In Revelation 5 John witnesses the ascension and triumphant return of Christ to heaven after his great victories. The mighty Lion of Judah is, amazingly, also the Lamb who was slain (Rev 5:5–6). He alone is worthy to bring about God's purposes on earth (Rev 5:9–10) and the chapter ends with the worship of the one on the throne and of the Lamb (Rev 5:11–14).

Heaven exists now, but is it a place or a dimension beyond space and time? We cannot be dogmatic here. God is a Spirit as are the angels who worship him in heaven. Solomon rejoiced that in some way God came to dwell in the temple he had built, and yet was conscious that this was something of a mystery and a paradox:

> "But will God really dwell on earth? The heavens, even the highest heaven, cannot contain you. How much less this temple I have built!" (1 Kings 8:27)

God is everywhere at once in the fullness of his being (Psalm 139:7–14). He both permeates his creation and transcends it. How can he be the God who dwells in heaven? Surely there is symbolism here in Revelation 5 but there are other considerations we need to entertain before we dismiss the idea. This third heaven is the place to which Enoch and Elijah were taken. More than that, Jesus returned to heaven in his resurrection body. This body did not evaporate or vaporize but returned to the throne room of God. The physical body of the God-man, Jesus Christ, can only be in one place at once, and that one place is the throne room of heaven where he sits at the Father's right hand. One day he will return in bodily form to this earth, but at this moment in time he is located in heaven.

Heaven is a real place and it exists now. Where is it? God does not choose to give us the answer to that question.

Question two: Do Christians go straight to heaven when they die?

Human beings are made up of two parts – body and soul. The body is physical and the soul is non-physical. They belong together and are essential to our nature as humans. Death is the unnatural and horrific ripping apart of the body and soul. The Christian hope is for the resurrection of the body when these two essential elements of our being are reunited forever. The resurrection of Christ is the model of our resurrection which will occur when he returns. Our future existence is a bodily existence. Our hope is for the resurrection of the body not just the immortality of the soul.

But what happens to the souls of believers between physical death and bodily resurrection? When my dad died this was one of the first questions I wanted an answer to.

Death is often referred to as a sleep, and the body is laid to rest (1 Thess 4:13–15). But we should not be misled by this. It is the body which sleeps, not the soul. The moment the soul of a believer leaves their body it enters into the presence of Christ and begins to enjoy all the glories of heaven. One day the body will be "re-wakened", but the soul is already conscious.

In 2 Corinthians 5:8, Paul tells us that he would prefer to be away from the body and at home with the Lord. He expresses himself even more strongly when writing to the Philippians:

> "For to me, to live is Christ and to die is gain. If I am to go on living in the body, this will mean fruitful labour for me. Yet what shall I choose? I do not know! I am torn between the two: I desire to depart and be with Christ, which is better by far …" (Phil 1:21–23)

If death leads to an unconscious state this would seem a strange thing for Paul to long for. But he has a real and reliable expectation that he will be home and enjoying

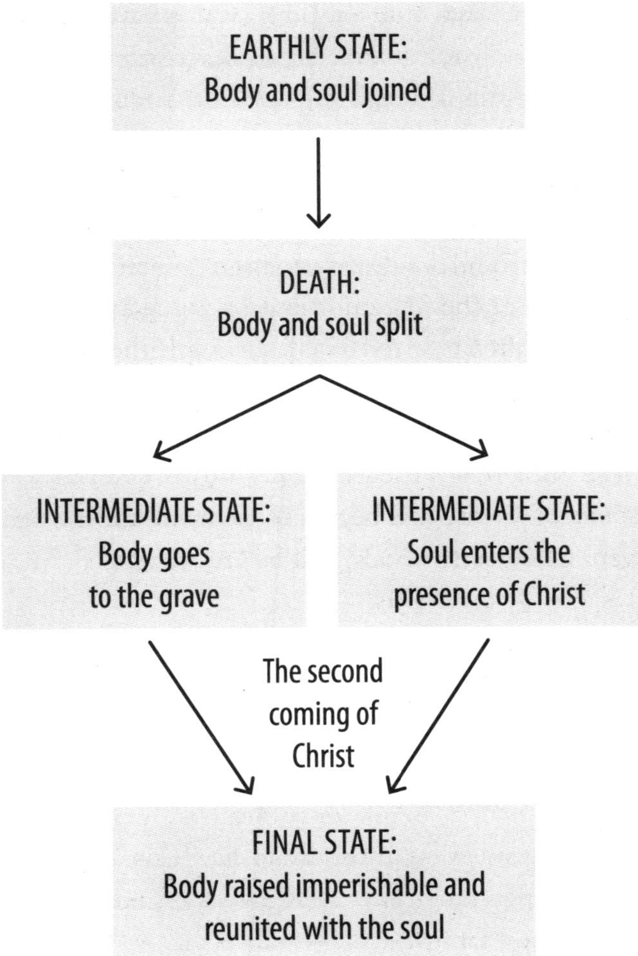

the presence of the Lord. After death, life is enhanced not diminished.

This is reinforced by the words of Jesus to the believing thief on the cross: "Truly I tell you, today you will be with me in paradise" (Luke 23:43).

The thief died and his body was probably thrown into a common grave. But his soul accompanied Christ into God's presence. The soul of Christ returned home between his death and resurrection, and then he ascended back there after forty days.

Paradise is not oblivion; it is a metaphor for heaven. It is a word derived from Persian and used to refer to "a walled park" or an "enclosed garden" where invited guests could walk with the king. As they wait for the resurrection, believers enjoy fellowship with the King of kings. Where are they? They are where Jesus is. And where is Jesus? He is in heaven.

This comes into sharper focus when we see the way in which Paul uses the word paradise:

> "I know a man in Christ who fourteen years ago was caught up to the third heaven. Whether it was in the body or out of the body I do not know – God knows. And I know that this man – whether in the body or apart from the body I do not know, but God knows – was caught up to paradise and heard inexpressible things, things that no one is permitted to tell." (2 Cor 12:2–4)

Paul is referring to his own experience although is reticent to describe it. The "third heaven" is God's dwelling place, his throne room, where Christ reigns with the Father. He identified this with "paradise" – they are one and the same.

We must not think of souls existing in heaven as having a kind of shadowy half-life. The dead in Christ are fully conscious and actively engaged with the glories around them. Perhaps, during this intermediate period, we will be like the angels. They are spiritual beings without bodies and yet they can see and speak and rejoice and worship God.

So we begin to experience the glories of heavenly existence at the moment of death, but this experience has two phases – phase one is to be with Christ awaiting the resurrection body; phase two is the full consummation of all heavenly joys when we receive the resurrection body.

There is life after life after death!

The essence of both phases is to be "with Christ". The longing for heaven is the longing for Christ. We might describe the hope of God's people in terms of good, better and best.

Good – this is the present state of the living, justified believer who is blessed with every spiritual blessing in Christ.

Better – this is the state of those who have died in Christ. They are with Christ and set free from all the sorrows, temptations and hardships of this world. They are in a better state than us, but they are awaiting the resurrection of the body, the creation of the new heaven and earth, and the final gathering together of all God's people.

Best – this is the final state when the soul and body are reunited, and the glorified saints rejoice in God's presence and serve him forever.

Question three: Where will heaven be in the future?

When a believer dies their soul goes to heaven to be in the presence of God, but this is not their final destination. They are waiting eagerly for the day of resurrection. From that day onwards they will spend eternity in this embodied existence, but where will they actually live?

A popular idea is that we are destined to spend eternity somewhere "out in space". It is a very other-worldly and ethereal existence with little connection to planet earth, which will be vaporized and cease to exist.

This is not what the Bible teaches.

In the penultimate chapter of the Bible, John describes the place where the saints will dwell forever:

> "Then I saw 'a new heaven and a new earth,' for the first heaven and the first earth had passed away, and there was no longer any sea." (Rev 21:1)

Elsewhere our future destination is described as "an enduring city" whose "architect and builder is God" (Heb 13:14; 11:10). The city is located in a better heavenly country (Heb 11:16).

There is debate about the location of this new creation, but I think the evidence points to it being this same universe but radically and splendidly transformed. It may be that the forces of nature like gravity and the speed of light will be modified in some way as this universe is made new but the next world will not be a strange and futuristic fantasy. It will be a wonderfully recognizable home:

> "We love this world because it is God's, and it will be healed, becoming at last what God intended from the beginning."[2]

What is my basis for saying Revelation 21:1–4 is not describing destruction and annihilation but re-creation and restoration?

The opening chapter of the Bible affirms the reality and importance of the physical universe. God created a material universe and said that it was good (Gen 1:31). Although it is marred, it continues to be good. The whole creation groans, longing for liberation and restoration (Rom 8:22–23). Jesus himself speaks of the "renewal of all things" (Matt 19:28) and Paul tells us that one day Christ will reconcile all things on earth and in heaven (Col 1:20), bringing unity to the whole creation (Eph 1:10).

The body of Christ was not abandoned but raised in a transformed state. The same will happen to our bodies. Surely the same will apply to the creation.

The word used for "new" in Revelation 21:1 has a range of meanings from totally new to totally renewed. Peter says that "the present heavens and earth are reserved for fire" (2 Pet 3:7), but this is not necessarily obliteration. Fire cleanses and purifies. Peter compares the future purification of the earth with the destruction brought by the flood in the days of Noah (2 Pet 3:6). However, the flood was an act of purification, not annihilation. After the waters receded, the creation remained, along with the times and seasons (Gen 8:22).

God won't abandon his universe. The devil tried to spoil it – he will not win. Rather, Satan will be defeated (John 12:31) and the meek will inherit the earth (Matt 5:5) and the church will reign on the earth (Rev 5:10).

One theologian puts it like this:

> "The planet was fashioned to be man's heritage … Satan sought to mar the divine plan, by the seduction of our first parents. For long ages he seemed to triumph … But Messiah will come and re-establish his throne in the midst of his scarred and ravaged realm; he will cleanse away every stain of sin and death and make the earth bloom forever with more than its pristine splendour …" [3]

John describes the new Jerusalem descending down from heaven and God himself being present with his people in the new creation (Rev 21:2–3). As heaven and earth unite, the earth will become the place where God has his kingly throne. The whole of the new creation becomes the temple of God.

So our final destiny is here on earth!

Our eternity will involve real mountains and rivers and forests. Our physical bodies will live in a physical place. The curse will be gone forever and this place of strife and pain will become a place of peace and joy.

Home is where our story begins and is where it will end.

Question four: What about those who aren't believers?

The book of Revelation paints a mouth-watering picture of heaven which is designed to strengthen the hearts of struggling Christians. However it also contains the most terrifying teaching about hell that we find anywhere in the Bible.

In Revelation 6:1–8 John sees the famous four horsemen who bring conquest, war, famine and death to the earth. Next comes a vision of the souls of those who have been martyred because they were faithful to God's Word and testified to its truth (Rev 6:9–11). They cry out for justice.

Finally we watch the cosmic events which result in the final judgement:

> "Then the kings of the earth, the princes, the generals, the rich, the mighty, and everyone else, both slave and free, hid in caves and among the rocks of the mountains. They called to the mountains and the rocks, 'Fall on us and hide us from the face of him who sits on the throne and from the wrath of the Lamb! For the great day of their wrath has come, and who can withstand it?'" (Rev 6:15–17)

The list covers every class of people in John's day – from kings to slaves. Judgement is universal. And it is so overwhelming that these people would prefer to be crushed by an avalanche than have to look upon the face of God. The mere glance of an angry God is dreadful. They also face the wrath of the Lamb. Those who do not trust Jesus as Saviour must face him as Judge. The passage ends with the plaintive cry, who can stand?

Jesus teaches in Matthew 25:31–46 that when he returns he will separate his sheep from those who rejected him during the final judgement. Those who didn't trust in the Saviour will be justly sent to hell. We are told: "Then they will go away to eternal punishment, but the righteous to eternal life" (Matt 25:46).

This terrifying eternity awaiting the unbeliever stands in stark contrast to the welcome Christians anticipate:

> "Then the King will say to those on his right, 'Come, you who are blessed by my Father; take your inheritance, the kingdom prepared for you since the creation of the world.'" (Matt 25:34)

At this point it would be remiss of me to fail to ask whether you have settled the matter. Have you trusted Jesus?

The choice is binary. Jesus is either your Saviour or he will be your Judge. The Saviour will welcome you into heaven; the Judge will condemn you to hell. There is no middle ground.

PART 2

GLIMPSING GLORY

One of the great joys of parenting can be the opportunity to have grandchildren. Not only do they make you feel younger – they also make you think about eternity. A considerable amount of their lives will be lived after you are gone.

My four-year-old grandson's favourite book is currently *The Snail and the Whale.* Boaz adores this story of friendship between a small gastropod and a large marine mammal. The snail hitches a lift on the back of the whale and explores a world he would never see otherwise. We follow his many adventures until, through no fault of its own, the whale is stranded on a beach. With the aid of children from a nearby school, the snail rescues his friend and they continue their adventures.

Although he's read the story many times, whenever we reach the crisis moment Boaz expresses his concern that the whale might not escape. Of course, the whale always does but I'm reminded each time that there are few things as tragic as a beached whale. Kind people can keep it alive for a while but its only hope is to return to the water. The water is a whale's element. In the water it lives and moves and has its being. Out of the water this magnificent creature will soon perish.

Human beings were created for a relationship with God. He is our element. In him we live and move and have our being. Without God we are stranded in an alien environment. Made in the image of God, human beings are still magnificent creatures, but they are cut off from the source of life. Salvation involves being reconnected with God. True life is always life in relationship with him.

And this will be the heart of our heavenly experience. In this section we will explore the nature of heaven as it is revealed in the Bible. But bear in mind that whatever else is said about heaven, without God as its central focus we remain like beached whales.

Even so we struggle to picture heaven because it is beyond our current knowledge and experience. It may even seem too good to be true. But Jesus is uniquely qualified to give us a glimpse of glory.

He is the eternal Son of God who has always existed in the embrace of his Father's love. When he came to earth he came from the presence of the Father, from heaven itself. He reminds Nicodemus:

> "I have spoken to you of earthly things and you do not believe; how then will you believe if I speak of heavenly things? No one has ever gone into heaven except the one who came from heaven – the Son of Man." (John 3:12–13)

Later, describing himself as the bread of heaven, he says:

> "For the bread of God is the bread that comes down from heaven and gives life to the world." (John 6:33)

Jesus knows what he is talking about!

But there is more.

He is the one man who has passed through the gates of death, conquered it and returned to tell the tale! Shakespeare speaks of the "undiscovered country" from which no traveller returns. But Jesus did! Jesus really died on the cross. For three days his body slept but his soul was with his Father. On the third day he rose and came back to his disciples as the one who has "destroyed death and has brought life and immortality to light through the gospel" (2 Tim 1:10). We know that during the forty days he was with them Jesus taught them about the kingdom of God (Acts 1:3). Presumably this would have included telling them what they needed to know about heaven.

Having ascended to heaven it was from there that he revealed the splendours of the new creation to his servant John. Revelation opens with these words: "The revelation from Jesus Christ, which God gave him to show his servants what must soon take place" (Rev 1:1).

Notice that this final book of the Bible is both a revelation *from* Jesus Christ and a revelation *of* Jesus Christ. He is both the infallible source and the sublime subject of the book. He stands at the centre of the renewed heaven and earth.

So away with agnosticism! Relying on the teaching of the Bible, and particularly that of Jesus and his apostles, we can approach this subject with confidence.

CHAPTER 5

A BODILY LIFE

Tom was one of the first guys I witnessed to as a young Christian. I was thirteen at the time and we were in the same class at school. We both loved James Bond movies and football. He was an Aston Villa fan, but then no one is perfect.

Tom was brought up as a Catholic but even at that age he doubted most of what he had been taught. He believed in God, but that was about it. We discussed pretty much every aspect of the Christian faith from the problem of suffering to the meaning of the cross to the trustworthiness of the Bible. I was an untaught apologist and I'm not sure that my answers were very persuasive, but I was able to talk about my own personal faith and Tom treated me with respect.

One day we talked about heaven. I cannot remember what I said but I remember Tom's take on the subject: "Heaven sounds so boring! It's like detention without your mates. And you have to be there forever."

It's not the first time I have heard that kind of verdict, though not in those words! George Bernard Shaw quipped:

> "Heaven as conventionally conceived, is a place so inane, so dull, so useless, so miserable, that nobody has ever ventured to describe a whole day in heaven, though plenty of people have described a day at the seaside."[1]

And listen to atheist Richard Dawkins:

> "And even if you do go to heaven; eternity in heaven – not just sitting in heaven for billions of years, but trillions of years (these are timespans beyond our comprehension) [imagine] how unbelievably boring it would be."[2]

Are they right?

Floating on a cloud

Think of the cartoons and comedy sketches of heaven you have seen. Think of some of the great paintings of Western art. In the popular imagination, heaven is perceived as a kind of non-material dream-like existence. It is somewhere out there – another dimension of existence characterized by clouds and mist with perhaps some stringed instruments and Gregorian chants thrown in for good measure. In this ethereal dimension we float from cloud to cloud in a disembodied ghost-like state.

It seems logical. God is spirit so why on earth would we need a body to dwell with him forever? And, since the body quickly deteriorates after death, isn't it stretching our credulity to believe that it can somehow be revived or restored? What would we even gain by expecting a physical existence? After all, isn't my soul the real me? Surely the real Christian hope is the immortality of the soul rather than the resurrection of the body?

The answer to all these questions is an emphatic "No!"

Greek philosophy vilified the body as the prison cell which entombed the mind. Liberation involved escaping from this tomb. This is why the intelligentsia of Athens sneered when Paul preached the resurrection of Jesus (Acts 17:32). But Paul was being faithful to the Scriptures when he proclaimed the resurrection of the dead.

As we have seen, the Bible speaks of a new heaven and earth. The next world is not a strange and futuristic fantasy but a wonderfully recognizable home. It is a renewed physical earth where God dwells in the new Jerusalem with his people. So we are certainly not looking for a non-material dreamworld.

John Piper summarizes it like this:

> "What happens to our bodies and what happens to the creation go together. And what happens to our bodies is not annihilation but redemption … Our bodies will be redeemed, restored, made new, not thrown away."[3]

In this physical heaven we will have physical bodies.

Keeping body and soul together

Scientific materialism teaches that physical matter is the only thing that exists and that humans must be explained in terms of matter alone. We may be the most sophisticated creatures in the universe, but in the final analysis we are merely machines made out of meat. There is no invisible spiritual element in people – no ghost in the machine.

The Bible views humans very differently.

Human beings are the result of a conscious, deliberate and purposeful act of God. God created Adam with care and for a specific purpose. He was created at the same time as the animals and is therefore a creature. However he stands apart from other creatures because he has been created in the image of God. He alone is capable of a conscious personal relationship with God. Unlike the animals he has an invisible dimension – he is soul as well as body. He stands apart from the animals because he has a non-physical soul as well as a physical body.

Therefore we consist of two elements – one physical and the other non-physical.

This is hinted at in the creation account:

> "Then the LORD God formed a man from the dust of the ground and breathed into his nostrils the breath of life; and the man became a living being." (Gen 2:7)

Man was created by an act of special creation and personal intimacy – God kisses him into existence. Into the physical dust, God himself breathes life.

Our bodies are essential to our make-up. We are undeniably material beings. Any view which denigrates the body is contrary to biblical Christianity. The body is not a prison, but a wonderful piece of art created by the hand of God:

> "For you created my inmost being;
> you knit me together in my mother's womb.
> I praise you because I am fearfully and
> wonderfully made;
> your works are wonderful,
> I know that full well." (Psalm 139:13–14)

There is nothing despicable or sinful about matter. The visible world is a lush and beautiful revelation of God. The incarnation of the Son of God proves that the body is not essentially evil in itself. The early Christians emphasized this against the false teachers who denied that God had come in the flesh (John 1:14; 1 John 4:2–3).

The body and the soul are distinct but they belong together. Every act we perform is an act of our whole being. It is not the soul or the body that acts but the whole person. Death occurs when the unity of the body and soul is temporarily disrupted (Ecc 12:7; 1 Thess 4:13–18). To be separated is abnormal. That is why the intermediate state can only be temporary.

Paul tells us that the physical body is like a tent which has seen better days (2 Cor 5:1–3)! We groan and long for release from the inevitable decay and decline that our earthly bodies are subject to:

> "For while we are in this tent, we groan and are burdened, because we do not wish to be unclothed but to be clothed instead with our heavenly dwelling, so that what is mortal may be swallowed up by life." (2 Cor 5:4)

Though there will be a period when we are not "clothed" in either our old or new body, our real hope is for "our heavenly dwelling" – our new resurrection body.

The resurrection of Christ

Christ came in the flesh, lived in a body, and died when his body and soul separated. He rose again when this same body was reunited with his soul on the third day.

Perhaps the most detailed account of his resurrected state is found in Luke's Gospel:

> "While they were still talking about this, Jesus himself stood among them and said to them, 'Peace be with you.'
>
> They were startled and frightened, thinking they saw a ghost. He said to them, 'Why are you troubled, and why do doubts rise in your minds? Look at my hands and my feet. It is I myself! Touch me and see; a ghost does not have flesh and bones, as you see I have.'
>
> When he had said this, he showed them his hands and feet. And while they still did not believe it because of joy and amazement, he asked them, 'Do you have anything here to eat?' They gave him a piece of broiled fish, and he took it and ate it in their presence." (Luke 24:36–43)

Luke, a medical doctor, is at great pains to marshal all the evidence which proves that the person the disciples met on the first Easter evening was the same Jesus they had known and followed for three years.

The disciples are numb with grief. Their hopes have been crushed and their dreams have become a nightmare. They are shattered men. Jesus is dead and dead men don't rise. Then a series of shocking stories begin to circulate about empty tombs and angelic visitations and sightings of a dead man walking.

As they discuss these rumours Jesus himself stands among them. Their first reaction is instinctive and understandable. They are terrified and think they are seeing a ghost. Jesus speaks peace into their hearts and then proves that he is physically present and very much alive. As evidence he appeals to their physical senses.

They can see him with their own eyes. He does not appear at a distance on a hillside surrounded by mist. He is up close and personal. He invites them to look at his hands and his feet. They are the same hands and feet that were nailed to a cross. It is the same body not an illusion or a mirage or a bodiless ghost.

They can hear him with their own ears. He reasons with them as he had done so often before. In the words of The Message version of the New Testament:

> "Don't be upset, and don't let all these doubting questions take over. Look at my hands; look at my feet

> – it's really me. Touch me. Look me over from head to toe. A ghost doesn't have muscle and bone like this."

Jesus probably spoke with a Galilean accent. The timbre of his voice would have been familiar. It was the same man speaking to them.

He invited them to touch him. The Greek word suggests not a light touch, but a firm grasp. Although Luke does not tell us that they took Jesus up on his invitation, I'm convinced that they did. After all when the disciples told Thomas, his response was to request the same evidence that they had received:

> "Unless I see the nail marks in his hands and put my finger where the nails were, and put my hand into his side, I will not believe." (John 20:25)

He wants to touch Jesus' scars – suggesting that they reported how they had done the same. And even that is not enough. As a clinching argument Jesus eats a piece of fish in front of them – a kind of piscatorial apologetics.

Jesus' resurrection body is a speaking, eating, touchable one. But what is the significance of this for our hope of heaven?

At the very least it proves the importance of the body. At the incarnation the Son of God took a complete body and soul to himself. He is now and always will be the God-man. When he ascended to heaven Jesus' body did not dematerialize and become "non-fleshly". The angels assured the disciples that Jesus "will come back in the same way you have seen him go into heaven" (Acts 1:11). Jesus was not a ghost then and he is not a ghost now. He had, and has, a physical size and shape and even a physical appetite. Such things can exist in heaven. But will they exist for us?

The firstfruits

Imagine a field of tulips in the early spring. Most of the flowers are yet to bud but by some accident of nature in one field they have developed early bringing into existence a blaze of amazing colour. What is visible in this one field will soon be evident everywhere.

Christ's resurrection is like a blaze of glory which will be repeated in our resurrection bodies. His resurrection body is the template for his people. He will "transform our lowly bodies so that they will be like his glorious body" (Phil 3:21). He has gone before us and we will follow:

> "But Christ has indeed been raised from the dead, the firstfruits of those who have fallen asleep." (1 Cor 15:20)

And John teaches the same:

> "Dear friends, now we are children of God, and what we will be has not yet been made known. But we know that when Christ appears, we shall be like him, for we shall see him as he is." (1 John 3:2)

His resurrection is a foretaste of our resurrection. Notice three things.

1. We will have a real body

Just as the disciples came to see that it was a real man with "flesh and bones" standing in front of them, our eternal bodies will be real bodies. We too will have flesh and bone and blood and sinews. We will be spellbound by magnificent music and gaze on stunning vistas. We will enjoy exotic new tastes and scent pleasing aromas. We will feel the wind in our hair and the solid ground under our feet. I hope I am not allowing my imagination to run away with me – but that's what physical bodies do! We will be real physical people inhabiting a real physical new creation. Of course natural laws might work slightly differently, but we're not looking towards an insubstantial, floating-on-clouds existence. For a start, physical bodies are heavier than clouds!

2. We will have the same body

As we have seen human beings are soul *and* body creatures. Our bodies are integral to who we are, and the idea that they will become in some way redundant or disposable is unbiblical. It is therefore a glorious truth that on the resurrection morning we will regain everything, including our bodies – the very same one we currently inhabit.

There was a recognizable continuity between Jesus' earthly body and his risen body. This was the whole point of the empty tomb. Jesus' body had not somehow dissipated or disappeared – it had risen. He showed the disciples his scars (Luke 24:39) and invited them to touch his wounds (John 20:24–28). His followers may not always have recognized him at first but this was because "they were kept from recognising him" (Luke 24:16). On other occasions they quickly knew him (Matt 28:9,17; John 20:19–20,26–28; 21:7,12).

And, again, Jesus is our pattern:

> "For the Lord himself will come down from heaven, with a loud command, with the voice of the archangel and with the trumpet call of God, and the dead in Christ will rise first." (1 Thess 4:16)

Paul died two thousand years ago and in all likelihood there are no physical remains of his body still in existence. And yet Paul was confident that, however long till Christ's return, his own body would rise from the dust.

Only God knows how this will happen. Our physical bodies change during our lifetimes but our DNA, our personalities and our unique characteristics remain the same. At sixty-seven my body is different from what it was when I was twenty-seven or forty-seven, but it is still my body.

What will be the apparent age of resurrection bodies? The Bible does not answer this question. I became a Christian at the age of eleven. If I had died shortly after, would my resurrection body be that of an eleven-year-old? Probably not! Let's wait and see!

3. We will have a transformed body

The body of Jesus was not like the body of Lazarus, who rose only to die again. Jesus did not simply come back from the dead. His new body had new properties and possibilities. He could suddenly appear (John 20:19,26) or disappear (Luke 24:31). In this body he was able to ascend to heaven (Acts 1:9).

We need bodies with new properties in order to enjoy eternal life:

> "In its present fallen condition, this body cannot withstand the glory of the heavenly city; it must be glorified, as Christ's body was, in order to participate in the age to come. Flesh and blood in its present, fallen condition cannot endure the joys of Zion … We cannot imagine the glory of our future existence, but we can look to Christ as our forerunner."[4]

So what will this new body be like?

All change

Paul describes the nature of the resurrection body in his letter to the church in Corinth:

> "The body that is sown is perishable, it is raised imperishable; it is sown in dishonour, it is raised in glory; it is sown in weakness, it is raised in power; it is sown a natural body, it is raised a spiritual body." (1 Cor 15:42–44)

Without denying the continuity between our current bodies and our resurrection bodies, Paul shows the radical discontinuity by a series of contrasts.

Our present bodies are marked by corruption – they are "perishable". Because of the curse, we carry the seeds of decay and death within us from the moment of conception. Our bodies are liable to disease and injury; cancer and depression. As we get older we face the increased possibility of hearing loss, cataracts, osteoarthritis, pulmonary disease and dementia. Old age does not come alone! Our faces bear the marks of time.

The resurrection body, however, is incorruptible. It will never perish or feel the ravages of time. It will never again be touched by decay, disease or death. Can you imagine what it will be to have the wisdom of age and the strength of youth?

Not only are our bodies currently perishable, they are "dishonourable". Not that physical bodies are bad, but at present they are marked by sin and unrighteousness. They fail to come close to God's glory.

But the new body will be marked by glory as it partakes of the divine nature (John 17:22; 2 Pet 1:4). The word glory is used to describe the radiance that surrounds God's presence. Does this suggest that we will have a certain radiance in our resurrection bodies? Jesus said that "the righteous will shine like the sun in the kingdom of their Father" (Matt 13:43). And in Daniel we read:

> "Those who are wise will shine like the brightness of the heavens; and those who lead many to righteousness, like the stars for ever and ever." (Dan 12:3)

When Moses came from the presence of God his face shone because he had seen God's glory. We will have a closer fellowship with God than even Moses enjoyed. Perhaps there will be some new physical magnificence. At the very least we will be free from every taint of sin and evil forever.

The present body is marked by "weakness". Weakness is part and parcel of our human condition. My wife has been in a wheelchair for thirty-two years. My dad died in his sixties. My mother-in-law lost both her legs as a result of diabetes. One of my grandsons has a profound and life-limiting neurological condition. And this is just one family. In all our activities we are aware of our human frailty and limitations. Like Paul we know that we have the treasure of the gospel in earthen vessels (2 Cor 4:7).

In wonderful contrast, the resurrection body is characterized by "power". All decay and frustration are gone forever. This body will have new stamina and speed and durability. Will we have new unimagined capacities? Maybe! But we cannot go beyond what the Bible says, so we will have to wait and see.

Joni Eareckson Tada enjoyed a very full life until a dreadful accident aged seventeen left her as a tetraplegic. She writes of the new body:

> "I can hardly believe it. I, with shrivelled, bent fingers, atrophied muscles, gnarled knees, and no feeling from the shoulders down, will one day have a new body, light, bright, and clothed in righteousness – powerful and dazzling. Can you imagine the hope this gives someone spinal-cord injuries like me? ... No other religion, no other philosophy promises new bodies, hearts and minds. Only in the gospel of Christ do hurting people find such incredible hope."[5]

We have a "natural body" now marked out by weakness, frailty, powerlessness and vulnerability. As Christians we still struggle with temptation and failure, we grapple with doubts and fears and we wrestle with pain and death. We know it is not supposed to be like this, but we are still caught up in this world with all its limitations.

After the resurrection we will have a "spiritual body". On the surface this may appear to suggest that the resurrection body will be non-physical, composed of spirit rather than flesh. However, this would be to misunderstand Paul's meaning. Paul has already used the terms natural and spiritual in 1 Corinthians 2:14–15. Here the "natural" person belongs to the present age and is susceptible to its pressures. The "spiritual" person is one who is guided by the Holy Spirit. Our future resurrection body will also be animated and empowered by the Spirit. This body will always be in tune with the Holy Spirit and his leading. It belongs to the age to come.

Thanks be to God

So this is our hope – a joyful hope of a new bodily existence superseding anything we have ever known before.

Listen to Robert Letham:

> "Resurrection is not the mere resuscitation of a corpse, returning to the same state as before. It is far greater in kind … No wonder the early church prayed standing and facing the east, the direction from which Christ was to return, in eager anticipation."[6]

And now Timothy Keller:

> "The resurrection of the body means that we do not merely receive a consolation for the life we have lost but a restoration of it. We not only get the bodies and lives we had but the bodies and lives we wished for but had never before received."[7]

And lastly listen to Paul as he writes some of the most exciting words in the Bible:

> "Listen, I tell you a mystery: we will not all sleep, but we will all be changed – in a flash, in the twinkling of an eye, at the last trumpet. For the trumpet will sound, the dead will be raised imperishable, and we will be changed. For the perishable must clothe itself with the imperishable, and the mortal with immortality. When the perishable

has been clothed with the imperishable, and the mortal with immortality, then the saying that is written will come true: 'Death has been swallowed up in victory.'

> 'Where, O death, is your victory?
> Where, O death, is your sting?'

The sting of death is sin, and the power of sin is the law. But thanks be to God! He gives us the victory through our Lord Jesus Christ." (1 Cor 15:51–57)

Hallelujah! Bring it on!

CHAPTER 6

A SOCIAL LIFE

During the Falklands War in 1982, the BBC correspondent Brian Hanrahan reported from the South Atlantic on board the aircraft carrier HMS Hermes. Describing an air strike by Harrier jump jets he got around reporting restrictions with the words:

> "I'm not allowed to say how many planes joined the raid, but I counted them all out, and I counted them all back. Their pilots were unhurt, cheerful and jubilant, giving thumbs up signs."

Christians also live in the middle of a war zone, but they have been sealed and they are secure. God knows their exact number and he will count them safely in! Every last one!

Not one will be lost.

We see this truth in Revelation 7 which contains two pictures of God's people. First, in verses 1 to 8, God's people are on earth in the middle of battle and then, in verses 9 to 17, they are in heaven resting after their labours. John sees four angels holding back the winds of judgement and then another angel appears:

> "He called out in a loud voice to the four angels who had been given power to harm the land and the sea: 'Do not harm the land or the sea or the trees until we put a seal on the foreheads of the servants of our God.'" (Rev 7:2–3)

A similar picture is found in Ezekiel 8–9. As God pronounces judgement on Jerusalem for its idolatry, he puts a mark on the foreheads of "those who grieve and lament over all the detestable things that are done in it" (Ezek 9:4). In both places the mark indicates that they belong to God and that he will keep them safe. Just like slaves were sealed with a master's mark to show that they were his property, those receiving the mark are God's servants. The number of those sealed is announced: 144,000 (Rev 7:4).

The roll call of these sealed ones is reminiscent of the numbering of the tribes in the book of Numbers. This imagery is deliberate. Israel had a census in order to know how many men would be drafted into the army. God's people are set for war.

The number 144,000 has caused much speculation and guesswork. I don't want to be dogmatic, but I suggest that it indicates fullness. Remember that numbers often have symbolic significance in biblical thinking. Ten is the number of completeness. God created the world by speaking ten times and he gave Israel his ten commandments. Ten to the power three is 1,000 – super completeness if you like.

Twelve refers to God's people. There were twelve tribes and twelve apostles. Twelve squared is 144, which multiplied by 1,000 gives us 144,000. This number therefore speaks of the fullness or completeness of God's people. And they are all sealed. They are all safe. God will preserve *all* his people.

Personal but not private

A popular concept of heaven is of solitary communion between the soul and God. In chapter 9 we will explore the intimacy of our relationship with Father, Son and Holy Spirit. This connection is at the very core of what the Bible teaches about heaven.

But, although the experience of heaven is intensely personal, it is not private. God's purpose has always been to save a people, not just a set of individuals. The church is more than a collection of those who find it convenient to meet together to strengthen their faith and pool their resources. Rather the church is a foretaste now of the multicultural people of God who will enjoy both God and one another for eternity.

The church is the bride for which Christ died and for whom he is preparing an eternal home. There will be one flock (John 10:16; 17:21), and one church of the firstborn (Heb 12:22–23). We will meet the Lord *together* (1 Thess 4:17). For those who feel acutely the sting of bereavement and separation, there is the promise of reunion with those of our loved ones who have died in Christ – we are to comfort each other with this prospect (1 Thess 4:13–18).

Thus one of the greatest joys of heaven will be the fellowship we enjoy for eternity. I look forward to seeing my mum and dad again. I want to thank so many of those who impacted my life for good, like my youth leader Robin and my pastor Les. I want to meet those people who have prayed for me. I want to meet Charles Spurgeon – I still read his sermons over 150 years since he preached them and they bless my soul. I want to meet the great characters of the Bible and the heroes of church history. Think of all the joys you have ever experienced through Christian fellowship. They are merely a flimsy foretaste of the fellowship of heaven.

Some Christians struggle with this. Church is supposed to be a place where we learn to grow as Christians but perhaps your experience of fellowship has been less than encouraging. Sadly it can easily become a place where we are damaged, discouraged and hindered from following Christ. Church can become toxic. The idea of spending eternity with people who have hurt us is difficult to cope with. However in the future all hurts, including emotional hurts, will be healed. With the scars gone we will be able to worship together with all God's people. In heaven we will be able to perfectly fulfil God's two great commandments: to love him with all our heart and soul and strength and mind, and to love our neighbour as ourselves.

Gathered in

We see this as we move into the second part of the vision. No longer on earth's bloody battlefield, we are transported to heaven where the throne of the Lamb is at the centre:

> "After this I looked, and there before me was a great multitude that no one could count, from every nation, tribe, people and language, standing before the throne and before the Lamb. They were wearing white robes and were holding palm branches in their hands." (Rev 7:9)

Unlike in the first half of Revelation 7, the emphasis is not on the exactness of their number but its vastness. They are a "great multitude" which cannot be counted. Just as Israel was to be as numerous as the stars and the sand on the seashore (Gen 22:17), so these people are so abundant that their number is beyond estimation.

And they are a cosmopolitan people from every corner of the earth. Retaining their own language and culture, they do not lose their distinctiveness, and yet they are fully united. The command of Jesus to make disciples of all nations will be fulfilled in this glorious multicultural people of God.

Living in a city like Birmingham I have preached in several multicultural churches. Experiencing worship with people from different cultures, enjoying their musical styles and understanding their life stories is incredibly enriching. This will only be multiplied as part of our heavenly experience. All barriers of race and culture and class will be effaced forever.

They are also a specific people:

> "These are they who have come out of the great tribulation; they have washed their robes and made them white in the blood of the Lamb." (Rev 7:14)

Here we come to the answer to the question at the end of Revelation 6. Who can stand in the presence of the Lamb who is the dreadful Judge of the whole earth? The answer is those with white robes. How did their robes become white? They washed them in the blood of the Lamb.

This sounds counter-intuitive and even slightly grotesque to our ears, but again the symbolism is vital to understanding the Bible's message. The blood of the Lamb represents the life of Christ poured out on the cross. We have no holiness of our own, indeed we are mired in the filth of sin. He died in the place of sinners in order to secure their forgiveness – their sins which were as red as crimson are now as white as snow (Isa 1:18).

By an amazing exchange Christ removes every stain of sin and clothes us in his own perfect righteousness. God looks on us and sees Christ's perfection. The Father welcomes the bride his Son has chosen into the eternal joys of the family banquet (Matt 26:29; Luke 14:15; Rev 19:9).

I have a large family and every time our family gathers we eat together. Can you imagine the joy of sitting at the Lord's table with all God's people? Can you imagine the new relationships to develop and the new stories to tell? But most of all Christ will be physically present in his resurrection body as the host at the head of the table. What an amazing prospect!

Some commentators explain this banquet in metaphorical terms and deny the necessity of eating food in the new creation. This may or may not be the case, but remember that in his resurrection body Jesus ate a piece of fish (Luke 24:41–43) and prepared breakfast for his disciples (John 21:1–14). This suggests that one of the joys of heaven will be feasting with God's people. Eating and drinking are not just functional. They are a source of great pleasure and an opportunity for corporate celebration.

Important questions

In my experience, discussing the way in which we relate to each other in heaven raises a number of questions.

1. Will we know each other in heaven?

Many Eastern religions see the future in terms of the annihilation of the self and its absorption into the infinite. Christianity is very different. After death we do not lose our personality or our personhood. In new bodies, we are still us. And we're still recognizable.

When Jesus was transfigured, Moses and Elijah appeared with him and they were recognized (Matt 17:3–4). On resurrection morning we will be like Jesus. After some hesitation, his disciples recognized him. He was the same Jesus they had known before he had died. In our transformed bodies we will also be somehow recognizable as the same people who lived on earth.

In 1 Thessalonians 4:14–18 Paul comforts bereaved Christians by telling them that they will be together with the Lord in heaven. This would not bring much comfort if we do not know each other in heaven. Paul says that one of the great joys of eternity will be to resume fellowship with his friends, especially those he has led to the Lord:

> "For what is our hope, our joy, or the crown in which we will glory in the presence of our Lord Jesus when he comes? Is it not you? Indeed, you are our glory and joy." (1 Thess 2:19–20)

Being able to see our believing loved ones will be one of the great blessings of heaven. Together we will enjoy God forever.

But it is more than just our loved ones. We will come to know Abraham and David; Mary, Peter and Paul; Martin Luther, Amy Carmichael and Elisabeth Elliot! We will meet a host of unknown believers whose lives left no footprints in history, but who have their own stories of faith to tell. We will meet those we have never met, but who prayed for us because our names appeared on a list of prayer needs somewhere.

Remember that the numbers in heaven are vast. We spend our lifetime getting to know a few people. But we have eternity to know and love this great crowd of saints.

2. Will we be male and female in heaven?

There are good grounds for believing that we will continue to be male and female in heaven.

The Bible says that we will be like the angels (Matt 22:30), but this does not necessarily mean that we will be gender-less. We will be similar to angels in that we will not marry. However there is one fundamental difference – angels are spirits and they are without bodies; we are both spiritual and physical. We have seen our bodies are as important as our souls – they belong together. Jesus' resurrection body continued to be masculine and he appeared to his disciples as a man.

Our bodies have clear biological sexual characteristics which match our gender. If gender is fundamental to our bodies and our bodies are fundamental to our future existence, it stands to reason that this will be a gendered existence.

Currently, there are many reasons why we may dislike our bodies. In some cases this may even lead to the pain of gender dysphoria. This will be healed in heaven.

3. Will there be marriage in heaven?

Married couples are heirs together of life (1 Pet 3:7). However, although there will be gender in heaven, it is clear that the marriage bond will cease. Jesus affirmed this:

> "At the resurrection people will neither marry nor be given in marriage; they will be like the angels in heaven ..." (Matt 22:30)

Marriage points forward to something greater than itself. In God's plan and design marriage on earth is a foretaste of the marriage supper of the Lamb. Here Christ is joined with his bride forever. The best marriages on earth are merely a faint foretaste of the intimacy which will exist between Christ and his people in the glory of heaven.

The pleasure of sexual intercourse will pass away to be replaced with something far better. When we experience the superlative pleasures of heaven, the pleasures of earth will look black and white compared to the technicolour of glory.

John Frame expresses it like this:

> "Our earthly families will be transcended by the worldwide family of God. But doubtless the new creation is not a time of lesser intimacy, but of greater intimacy with God and with other members of his body ... I don't know what will replace sexual pleasure, but I know that our intimacy with God and one another will be something greater and better than anything we know and enjoy on this earth – as everything will be."[1]

Whatever our relationship status is on earth, we will all feel fully connected and satisfied in heaven.

But how can we enjoy heaven when the people we love are not there?

This book is about heaven but if we believe in heaven we must also believe in hell. Every person we meet has an eternal destiny – it is just about the most important thing about them. They will spend eternity either in heaven or in hell. Many Christians find that they cannot fully enjoy the prospect of heaven because people they love are not yet saved. I must confess that I approach this subject with fear and trembling. Anyone who can be blasé about the fate of lost people has either a soft head or a hard heart.

All of us probably know at least one person for whom this is a painful dilemma. I have even met people who resisted becoming Christians because they thought that in eternity they would be separated from the people they loved.

In my first term at university I began to really struggle with the doctrine of hell. I felt dreadfully homesick, as many first-year students do, and this made me realize how much I loved my parents. My homesickness was compounded by the fact that mum and dad were not yet Christians. I loved them and I wanted to spend eternity with them. The idea of them going to hell was overwhelming. It broke my heart to know that they were lost and on a road leading to eternal conscious punishment.

A sympathetic friend tried to persuade me that I was worrying unduly. His view was that hell was a reality, but in the end very few, if any, people would end up there. I would have liked to believe this, but it's simply not what the Bible says. In particular it ignores the uncompromising teaching of Jesus.

In the end I was helped by Philip, a graduate researching his PhD in New Testament theology. I cannot remember everything Phil said, but he gave me some sound and helpful theology which was a balm for my troubled heart. He encouraged me not to surrender or compromise on what the Bible said about hell – to do so would be to be unfaithful to Christ. However he reminded me of two things.

Firstly, it is not a burden I or any other Christian believer can carry. Hell is real and we should care enough about people to share the gospel with them. Paul wished that he could be cut off so that the people he loved could be saved (Rom 9:1–4). If we can think about hell without tears in our eyes there is something wrong with us. However to bear the burden of a lost world is something we cannot do nor are we meant to. I am not the Messiah. Only Christ can bear this burden.

Secondly, he reminded me that I do not know the ultimate fate of any individual, but that the Bible seems to suggest that there will be more people in heaven than we ever imagined. There will be a great crowd that no one can count. We saw in chapter 3 that the dimensions of the new Jerusalem are stunning (Rev 21:16). I'm sure we're told the massive size to indicate this city will house a lot of people. "My Father's house has many rooms," comforts Jesus (John 14:2). And the Bible tells us that when our Saviour sees the fruit of his labours – all those that are saved – he will be satisfied (Isa 53:11).

It is important of course never to give false hope. Only those who have come to Christ in faith will be saved but we do not know the state of anyone's soul, even at the end of their lives. Yet we cannot consign any individual to hell. The God of all the earth will do what is right. Thankfully it is not our call. We have to leave our loved ones to the God who is full of grace and who will one day wipe all tears from our eyes.

It may be argued that in heaven we will not know of the existence of hell. However, this suggests an ignorance which the Bible does not teach. Jim Packer argues that because we will be transformed into the likeness of Christ, we will rejoice in the justice of God:

> "God will judge justly, and angels and saints and martyrs will praise him for it. So, it seems inescapable that we shall, with them, approve the judgement of persons – of rebels – whom we have known and loved."[2]

The martyrs cry out for justice (Rev 6:9–11). In heaven we will share their passion, not for revenge, but for the glory of God. With a new and clearer perspective we will see that all God's judgements are true and right and holy.

God is just in his very essence, acting according to a perfect internal standard of justice; he cannot do anything which is unjust. With God justice is not a habit, it is a perfection. In heaven we will be like God and we will be able to rejoice in the perfection of his justice. At the same time we will be amazed at grace and astonished that God, in justice, would punish his own Son to rescue us from hell. Our salvation will be a cause of eternal gratitude.

But at the present moment in time many of the people we love are still alive. If they are not saved we must do all in our power to win them for Christ. Pray and weep and point them to Christ.

My dad was saved when I was in my second term at university and my mum became a Christian thirty years later.

Don't give up!

CHAPTER 7

A LIFE OF REST

In the bitterly cold winter of 1647 Richard Baxter became ill with severe nosebleeds. This was put down to an excess of blood in the body, so his physicians opened his veins and bled him. Not surprisingly it almost killed him! Only in his early thirties, and expecting to die he wrote to a friend:

> "I was never yet nearly so low ... There is no other hope left: physicians, nature, flesh, blood, spirit, heart, friends all fail. But God is the strength of my heart and my portion forever."[1]

It caused him to think about heaven:

> "... far from home, cast into extreme languishing by the sudden loss of about a gallon of blood, I bent my thoughts on my everlasting rest."[2]

Baxter survived and lived into his seventies, but he never forgot that life was only a pilgrimage and that as Christians we should long for the rest which only heaven can bring:

> "What more welcome news to men under public calamities, unpleasing employments, plunderings, losses, sad tidings – which is common case – than this of Rest?"[3]

Life is a strenuous and dangerous voyage:

> "When we reach the harbour we have finished sailing. We will not need to fast, weep and watch anymore … it will be perfect freedom from all the evils that accompanied us through our whole course in this world …"[4]

The last battle has been fought and won and everything that causes pain or distress or heartache is gone forever as we enter the rest of heaven:

> "Nor is there such a thing as a pale face, feeble joints, languishing sickness, groaning fears, consuming cares or whatever deserves the name of evil. A gale of groans and a stream of tears will accompany us to the very gates and there they will bid us farewell forever."[5]

The loss of rest

The blessing of rest goes back to creation.

After God completes his work of creation he rests:

> "By the seventh day God had finished the work he had been doing; so on the seventh day he rested from all his work. Then God blessed the seventh day and made

it holy, because on it he rested from all the work of creating that he had done." (Gen 2:2–3)

This was not the rest of sleep or inactivity. God never slumbers nor sleeps and he cannot be exhausted (Psalm 121:4; Isa 40:28). This is rest from the particular work of creating – the creation was now complete and perfect. It was also the rest of enjoyment. He contemplates and delights in the work of his hands.

As a climax of creation God makes men and women in his image (Gen 1:26–28). He places them in the garden where they are "to work it and take care of it" (Gen 2:15). Life in the garden is life in the superlative. It is life in close and intimate fellowship with God. Adam and Eve walk with God in the cool of the day and all is well.

He also gives them the sabbath as a day to rest. As they rest they can enjoy what God has done through their labours. At this point work is uncursed and a delight to our first parents.

But then sin enters the picture.

They listen to the hiss of the serpent and entertain the idea that God is not as good as they imagined. Satisfaction can be found outside of God. Wanting to usurp God's position, they disobey his clear command in an act of reckless independence. Death enters the world – not just physical death but the broken relationship with God, which cuts them off from the source of life itself.

Like a flower cut at the stem, beauty soon fades and death touches their very existence.

They are exiled and become restless wanderers. This wandering life is exemplified by Cain who kills his brother and is cursed by God to be "a restless wanderer on the earth" (Gen 4:12).

The world is now like a beautiful but comprehensively damaged work of art.

There are still magnificent intimations of lost glory – the breath-taking sunset, heart-warming music or the soft touch of the lover's hand. But at the same time we are conscious that the masterpiece has been scarred with the graffiti of sin.

All our joys are touched with pain.

In grace God calls Abraham who becomes a pilgrim rather than a wanderer as he looks "forward to the city with foundations, whose architect and builder is God" (Heb 11:10). God brings his people to the Promised Land where they experience rest from their enemies (Josh 1:13; 21:44). They also experience the benefits of this rest in the reign of King David (2 Sam 7:1).

But sin again enters the picture.

The rest is lost, the kingdom is divided and the people are exiled. All seems hopeless, but the prophets promise a time when under God's chosen King the world will know rest, peace and justice:

> "Of the greatness of his government and peace
> there will be no end.
> He will reign on David's throne
> and over his kingdom,

> establishing and upholding it
> with justice and righteousness
> from that time on and for ever." (Isa 9:7)

The promise of rest

After years of waiting, Jesus appears, making amazing claims and offering staggering blessings:

> "Come to me, all you who are weary and burdened, and I will give you rest. Take my yoke upon you and learn from me, for I am gentle and humble in heart, and you will find rest for your souls. For my yoke is easy and my burden is light." (Matt 11:28–30)

This is the rest that the soul longs for. It is rest from the burdens and anxieties of this world. But it is much more.

Exile from Eden meant exile from God. But Christ restores this relationship. He takes our burdens upon himself and does all the heavy lifting. We find true rest in one who is gentle and humble in heart. And this is more than just the absence of cares and concerns, it is the positive enjoyment of all the good gifts that God has lavished on us in Christ.

This picture of the rest of salvation is taken up in Hebrews:

> "There remains, then, a Sabbath-rest for the people of God; for anyone who enters God's rest also rests

> from their works, just as God did from his. Let us, therefore, make every effort to enter that rest, so that no one will perish by following their example of disobedience." (Heb 4:9–11)

This culminates in the everlasting rest of heaven. Suffering is woven into our lives now. In heaven we will rest from all forms of agony and anguish. At last we will lay down our burdens and rest from all the struggles of life.

Battle and buffeting

We are headed for peace but currently we live in a battle zone. Paul describes this in Ephesians:

> "Finally, be strong in the Lord and in his mighty power. Put on the full armour of God, so that you can take your stand against the devil's schemes. For our struggle is not against flesh and blood, but against the rulers, against the authorities, against the powers of this dark world and against the spiritual forces of evil in the heavenly realms." (Eph 6:10–12)

The Christian life is not a picnic or a walk in the park. It is lived in the midst of a savage and ferocious battle. We do not struggle against mere flesh and blood. Behind persecution and temptation and many of our trials stands a living, intelligent, resourceful, malicious and violent foe. He dogs our footsteps all of the way. The Bible calls him the devil.

Peter describes him as a ferocious lion:

> "Be alert and of sober mind. Your enemy the devil prowls around like a roaring lion looking for someone to devour." (1 Pet 5:8)

Unlike the lions I saw as a child at Dudley Zoo, this lion is not lounging in the sun waiting to be fed. He is constantly on the prowl seeking an opportunity to destroy us.

Paul tells us that he "masquerades as an angel of light" (2 Cor 11:14). He is more crafty and cunning than us. We should not be surprised when he appears to be beautiful and persuasive.

John sees him as a great red dragon:

> "Then another sign appeared in heaven: an enormous red dragon with seven heads and ten horns and seven crowns on its heads. Its tail swept a third of the stars out of the sky and flung them to the earth." (Rev 12:3–4)

Think of the Tyrannosaurus Rex in *Jurassic Park* – his footsteps cause the ground to shake. Satan hates God's people and will do all that he can to destroy us. Don't expect any mercy. He hates our service for Christ, our church, our marriage, our children and all our longings for heaven.

Jesus Christ has dealt the death blow to Satan and all his malicious forces. In his life he crushed Satan's head (Gen 3:15; Rev 12:9). By his death he disarmed the powers and authorities and his resurrection sealed his victory (Col 2:15).

Satan is defeated. But he refuses to give up.

We live in that period of time between the Ascension and Return of Christ, when the dragon is "filled with fury, because he knows that his time is short" (Rev 12:12). There is no rest in this war.

In heaven the battle is over! The war is won:

> "And the devil, who deceived them, was thrown into the lake of burning sulphur, where the beast and the false prophet had been thrown. They will be tormented day and night for ever and ever." (Rev 20:10)

Satan is vicious but he is doomed. In the new creation he is eternally neutralized.

The world longs for peace and rest and it sometimes feels as if it is just round the corner. But of course it never is. War is part and parcel of the human experience. I write as war rages in Gaza and the Ukraine. There will only be peace when the prince of peace returns. And we long for peace in the spiritual battle.

But this will not happen till we reach heaven.

Once in heaven we will carry palm branches which are emblems of victory. Victory is total and complete. The long struggle is over; the battle is won; our wounds are healed.

The foe within

But we cannot blame the devil for everything.

What is the biggest battle you have to face as a Christian? Is it the battle against sickness or depression; the pain of bereavement or loneliness; the disappointment of a broken relationship or a financial loss?

The battle I have always found to be the most painful and challenging is the battle against sin. There are different opinions, but I think that this is what Paul is talking about in Romans when he says:

> "So I find this law at work: although I want to do good, evil is right there with me. For in my inner being I delight in God's law; but I see another law at work in me, waging war against the law of my mind and making me a prisoner of the law of sin at work within me. What a wretched man I am! Who will rescue me from this body that is subject to death? Thanks be to God, who delivers me through Jesus Christ our Lord!" (Rom 7:21–25)

Paul feels like a walking civil war. If you have ever felt like this, then welcome to the club!

We know the waywardness of our hearts and are often worn down by the daily tug of sinful desires. In Romans 8, Paul tells us that we can know a measure of deliverance from this internal civil war, as we live by the Spirit and put to death the deeds of the flesh (Rom 8:9–13). But the ultimate rest from this inner travail is in the new resurrection body where sin will be impossible.

The resurrected body is free from the physical and psychological limitations of its current experience. It is also free from the power and the presence of sin. One of the greatest joys of heaven is that not only will we never sin again but we will find it impossible to sin. We won't want to sin. We won't even want to want to sin![6]

Edward Donnelly puts it like this:

> "Never again will we break God's commandments. Never again will we fail our Saviour or cause pain to anyone. Never again will we have to beg for forgiveness. God has predestined us to be conformed to the image of his Son (Rom 8:29)."[7]

Reaching our rest

In the last chapter we spent some time thinking about the countless multitude who will enjoy the bliss of heaven (Rev 7:9). Before reaching eternity, however, they endured greatly for Christ:

> "These are they who have come out of the great tribulation; they have washed their robes and made them white in the blood of the Lamb." (Rev 7:14)

Jesus used the same word tribulation when he warned his disciples that they would have many tribulations in this world (John 16:33). Paul uses it when he tells the young churches in Asia Minor that they "must go through many hardships to enter the kingdom of God" (Acts 14:22). And Paul uses this word to describe his own experience:

> "We do not want you to be uninformed, brothers and sisters, about the troubles we experienced in the province of Asia. We were under great pressure, far beyond our ability to endure, so that we despaired of life itself. Indeed, we felt we had received the sentence of death." (2 Cor 1:8–9)

The Greek word means to crush, to hem in, to exert huge pressure. It was used of crushing olives in a press to extract oil or of squeezing grapes to obtain their juice.

This was the experience of those described in Revelation 7. They have known the extreme weight of persecution and hatred. Some have died as martyrs. Others have been despised and ridiculed for their faith. Their journey to heaven has not been an easy one. John pictures them as pilgrims. They have experienced the pangs of hunger and thirst and have felt the sun beating down on them.

John Bunyan was a contemporary of Richard Baxter. His great book *The Pilgrim's Progress* describes the journey to heaven, the "Celestial City". Christian faces opposition from his family and a host of others who will seek to discourage him and drive him from his path. He falls into swamps of despondency and is imprisoned in dungeons of doubt. He passes through Vanity Fair where the gaudy pleasures of the world seek to allure him. He is attacked by monsters and beaten half to death by vile foes.

The journey to heaven is hard and those who make it bear the scars. But in Revelation 7 all these things are gone, never to return. The pains of pilgrimage are over. They shelter in God's presence. They drink from the streams of living water. And God himself wipes all tears from their eyes.

The saints have entered into the rest of heaven.

In *The Pilgrim's Progress*, after many battles and not a few defeats, Christian finally reaches the river of death. It has been a long and painful journey and only the anticipation of this moment has helped him to persevere. At last the end of the journey is in sight.

As he reaches death however his faith begins to waver – the river is deep and cold. But his companion, Hopeful, urges him on. Then Christian sees the Lord Jesus across the river, reminding him of his promise that: "When thou passest through the waters, I will be with thee; and through the rivers, they shall not overflow thee."

And so Christian perseveres and finally reaches the gate of the Celestial City:

> "Now I saw in my dream that these two men went in at the gate; and lo, as they entered, they were transfigured, and they had raiment put on that shone like gold … Then I heard in my dream that all the bells in the city rang again for joy, and that it was said unto them, 'Enter ye into the joy of your Lord.' I also heard the men themselves, that they sang with a loud voice, saying,

> 'Blessing, and honour, and glory, and power, be unto him that sitteth upon the throne, and unto the lamb, forever and ever'."[8]

Amen! What a joy to rest in peace forever.

CHAPTER 8

A LIFE OF ACTIVITY

As a pastor I often visited care homes. Whenever I did this my wife would always remind me to make sure that I was not wearing a jumper! Even on a cold day these places tend to be heated like small greenhouses. It is no wonder the residents are often snoozing. I'm sure they deserve it – as I get older I appreciate more and more the blessings of sleep. But the rest of heaven is not a dream-like existence. Heaven is not a glorified rest home where the saints occasionally wake up and talk about their bunions before returning to the welcoming arms of slumber!

In heaven we will be more awake and more alive than we have ever been. It has been suggested that resurrection bodies may not need to sleep since Revelation 7:15 says: "... they are before the throne of God and serve him day and night in his temple."

Whether we sleep or not, if the descriptions in the book of Revelation are anything to go by, heaven will be a busy place full of activity, colour, noise, light and beauty. Yes we rest from our trials, burdens and heartaches. But we will continue to serve God.

But what does this service involve?

"Worship" and "worship"

Shortly after I had become a pastor I was invited to preach at another church and I decided to speak on the subject of worship from Psalm 100. I spoke about the psalmist's instructions on how we are to approach God, drawing near and singing songs of thanksgiving, celebration and praise. Worship is the total response of all I am to all that God has revealed of himself to me.

I have preached some controversial sermons in my time, but I was pretty sure this wasn't one of them. However at least one member of the congregation that morning did not agree.

Approaching me almost as soon as I had finished he took me to task. I don't remember his exact words but they were something like this:

> "What you said this morning was very misleading. I like singing, but that's not worship. Worship is what we do when we go to work on a Monday morning. It's what we do as husbands and as dads. It is our whole lives dedicated to God – not the hour on a Sunday when we sing a few songs."

I guess he was thinking of Paul's words in Romans 12:1 which urge us to worship with the totality of our lives – work, rest and play – dedicated to God. And he was certainly right that we can't divorce our worship in church from what we do the rest of the week. But it seems to me that the Bible uses the word worship in at least two senses.

In the widest possible sense worship does refer to everything we do. The prophets often castigate the people of God because their formal acts of worship – sacrifices and prayer – mask lives which are not lived to the glory of God. Instead of empty acts of sham adoration they should offer their lives to God:

> "He has shown you, O mortal, what is good.
> And what does the LORD require of you?
> To act justly and to love mercy
> and to walk humbly with your God." (Mic 6:8)

Worship is the dedication of the whole of my life to God. There are no no-go areas.

But worship is also used in a narrower sense. In fact this seems to be the Bible's more normal usage. Worship is the praise, adoration and reverent declaration of God's glory and the enthusiastic enjoyment of his goodness. Worship should be part of our private lives and the life of our family. We also gather together as church to worship God together.

When we sing, pray, confess our sins, hear God's Word read and preached, and celebrate the sacraments, we are engaged in worship. This is not merely a pit stop before we get on with the really important responsibilities of life. It is vital to our health and well-being as disciples of Jesus:

> "But you are a chosen people, a royal priesthood, a holy nation, God's special possession, that you may declare the praises of him who called you out of darkness into his wonderful light." (1 Pet 2:9)

Both understandings of worship are central to our nature as human beings and as Christians and both of them will be experienced to the full in heaven.

The heavenly court

My wife and I once attended a conference where three thousand Christians were gathered. On the last night we celebrated communion together. We had sung the last hymn and the benediction had been pronounced and there was a moment of profound silence. And then one brave individual in the congregation began to sing the words of a well-known song, "There is a Redeemer, Jesus God's own Son ..."

By the second line the congregation joined in. Without musical accompaniment three thousand voices sang of the amazing wonder of Calvary's love which we had just celebrated in bread and wine.

It was one of those moments when the spine tingles and the tears swell. It was a foretaste of heaven where a multitude of people join together in the worship of the triune God.

In Revelation 4 we glimpse the one who sits on the throne. God's glory is characterized by beauty, majesty and magnificence. His throne is established forever.

Around him is the heavenly court. It consists of the four living creatures which probably represent the whole of creation and the twenty-four elders which may symbolize all believers from all ages (twelve patriarchs and twelve apostles). Finally there are ten thousand times ten thousand angels – a hundred million angels who delight to adore the one on the throne.

In Revelation 5 the scene shifts to the scroll that is in the hand of God. It represents the unfolding of God's purposes in history. No one is found who is worthy enough or powerful enough to bring about these purposes and heaven weeps. But then we meet the Lion of Judah, the slain Lamb, Jesus Christ the Son of God. He is both worthy and able to bring all God's purposes to completion.

Heaven erupts with praise.

When we come to Revelation 7 we find the church – the great multitude – singing with the heavenly court. But there is one great difference. Angels sing about God's salvation as observers. We will sing of God's salvation as participants! Christ did not die and rise for angels; he did die and rise for his church.

The vast crowd cries out:

> "Salvation belongs to our God,
> who sits on the throne,
> and to the Lamb." (Rev 7:10)

For us worship is the spontaneous overflow of a joyful heart as it contemplates with wonder and astonishment the gift of God's Son to be our Saviour. The Lord of glory is the Lamb of Calvary who still bears the marks of nails on his hands and feet. The crowd wears white robes and waves palm branches which speak of celebration and joy. The worshippers do not hide in a corner and whisper "Isn't God good?", they shout in joyful acclamation.

In heaven, the service of worship never ends and never grows dull or wearisome.

Welcome to glory!

Joyful labour

But heaven is more than one long service of worship. In our resurrected bodies we will engage in physical, intellectual, creative and cultural pursuits, as Adam and Eve did before the Fall. Theologian Donald Macleod wrote:

> "Paradise [Eden] is no mere seminary where Adam and Eve whiled away the hours in theological discussion. I'm sure they did that, and they did it with more relish than any of my students. But Eden offered scope for art, science and technology as well as theology. The same will doubtless be true in the world to come."[1]

In Eden Adam and Eve worked the ground and enjoyed its fruits. They were active participants in the service of God's world. There is no suggestion that it will be different in heaven.

The Promised Land was the place of rest for Israel. It was also a place of joyful and fruitful labour. Heaven is not static. Wilbur Smith suggests that:

> "In heaven we will be permitted to finish those worthy tasks which we had dreamed to do while on earth but which neither time nor strength nor ability allowed us to achieve."[2]

Perhaps we will develop new skills unknown to us in the present age. These may include musical or artistic or technological or intellectual abilities which are as yet unrealized. The cultural mandate involves discovering the secrets and beauties of the new creation. Our supreme joy is in God, but this does not exclude rejoicing in the glories of his creation and gladly employing his gifts to tame and serve it.

Bruce Milne puts it like this:

> "The one who is Lord of the whole of life was never going to bring us at the end into an eternal existence of mental constriction, or of emotional and creative impoverishment. ... what creative possibilities await us in the unfolding of the eternal ages no present imagination can begin to unravel."[3]

If there is development, there may be some way in which we experience time in heaven. A physical body demands a time-space existence. Times and seasons will exist, and one event will follow another (Rev 21:24–26; 22:2). There will therefore be opportunities to grow and develop and to see old projects completed and new projects begun.

So, we will continue to work, but it will be a work which is free from toil and fatigue; work in which we take great delight and find satisfaction and fulfilment. The original cultural mandate is finally realized:

> "With the curse of sin gone, the apocalypses past, surely human beings will become active stewards of the Lord in completing or extending the universe of things and ideas. The whole creation groans, said Paul, awaiting human redemption. Civilization is not old: it has barely begun."[4]

Reigning with Christ

In Genesis 1:28 we see the original mandate given to Adam and Eve to act as God's co-regents on earth. Made in God's image they were to reign over the creation on his behalf and for his glory.

When they tried to usurp divine authority the universe was plunged into chaos and disorder but God's ultimate purpose is to "bring unity to all things in heaven and on earth under Christ" (Eph 1:10). This was accomplished through the death and resurrection of Christ – the last and better Adam. God's purpose was "through him [Christ] to reconcile to himself all things, whether things on earth or things in heaven, by making peace through his blood, shed on the cross" (Col 1:20).

At his enthronement, following his resurrection, Christ began a reign that will never end (Eph 1:20–23). This will be clearly established when he returns:

> "The kingdom of the world has become
> the kingdom of our Lord and of his Messiah,
> and he will reign for ever and ever." (Rev 11:15)

And amazingly, we are to reign with him! The ultimate calling of the church, Christ's bride, is to reign with her royal husband for eternity (Rev 22:5).

What does this mean for us? In the original creation account Adam acted as God's steward on earth. He named the animals showing that he had a God-given authority over them. Ruling over creation involves caring for it, enjoying its bounty and reflecting on God's glory as it is displayed in all that he has made. In the new creation we will reign over nature and the nations. Like so many things about heaven we have much to learn about how this will work out in a perfect curse-free world.

This reign is clearly promised in the book of Revelation. Encouraging persecuted believers Jesus promises:

> "To the one who is victorious and does my will to the end, I will give authority over the nations – that one 'will rule them with an iron sceptre and will dash them to pieces like pottery' – just as I have received authority from my Father." (Rev 2:26–27)

And again:

> "To the one who is victorious, I will give the right to sit with me on my throne, just as I was victorious and sat down with my Father on his throne." (Rev 3:21)

If we endure with him we will reign with him (2 Tim 2:12) as "co-heirs" (Rom 8:17).

It becomes even clearer in the last chapter of the Bible:

> "There will be no more night. They will not need the light of a lamp or the light of the sun, for the Lord God will give them light. And they will reign for ever and ever." (Rev 22:5)

And this seems to fit in with the rewards that Jesus refers to in his parables.

Rewards in heaven?

Consider the Parable of the Minas (Luke 19:11–27). Jesus is near Jerusalem where the religious leaders will reject his rule and crucify him because they do not want him to reign over them. In the future these enemies will be punished, but in the meantime he wants to prepare his disciples for his departure.

He is like a king who is going away for an indefinite period of time. In his absence they are entrusted with minas which they are to invest. A mina was a Greek coin worth around one hundred denarii or about four months' wages for an average worker. In the parable they could symbolize the gospel, the gifts of the Spirit or money. What did they do with what he has entrusted them with? The parable tells us that when the king returned he questioned each servant:

> "The first one came and said, 'Sir, your mina has earned ten more.'
>
> 'Well done, my good servant!' his master replied. 'Because you have been trustworthy in a very small matter, take charge of ten cities.'
>
> The second came and said, 'Sir, your mina has earned five more.'
>
> His master answered, 'You take charge of five cities.'"
>
> (Luke 19:16–19)

Faithful service is rewarded with further trust. Loyal and devoted labour for the king is repaid with the authority to reign. Christians must live their lives ready for the return of the King. One day we will stand before him and give an account. We will not lose our salvation but we can lose rewards.

Some people baulk at the idea of rewards. After all, salvation is the free gift of God and we are not saved on the basis of our merits, but because of all that Jesus did for us. There are no "degrees of salvation" and no first- and second-class Christians – we are equally lost and we are equally saved and the gospel destroys all distinctions.

God owes us nothing and heaven is a free gift based on a priceless sacrifice. The dying thief who trusted Christ entered into a full enjoyment of this inheritance (Luke 23:39–43) as much as the Apostle Paul who gave over years to missionary work. Eternal life is promised to all who believe, and this is unequivocal (John 3:16; Rom 2:7).

However the Bible does not shy away from the idea that we will receive rewards in heaven. This is one of the principal themes in the Sermon on the Mount. Think of how the sermon begins with the beatitudes (Matt 5:3–10). Why should a disciple persevere in the lifestyle described there? The answer is in order to receive rewards in heaven. The first and last beatitude promise the kingdom of heaven. In between we find a graphic picture of the heavenly life: it is a life of comfort, satisfaction, mercy and the vision of God. The meek will inherit the earth – the new creation.

The desire for treasure in heaven affects our hearts now, "For where your treasure is, there your heart will be also" (Matt 6:21).

Paul thinks of his service in terms of construction. Christ is building his church and Paul is part of the workforce. All Christians are called to be involved in this great project. How they do so will one day be tested. Every prayer I pray, every word of encouragement I offer and every act of kindness is part of this process. Paul warns that our service must be conducted with the right materials:

> "If anyone builds on this foundation using gold, silver, costly stones, wood, hay or straw, their work will be shown for what it is, because the Day will bring it to light. It will be revealed with fire, and the fire will test the quality of each person's work. If what has been built survives, the builder will receive a reward. If it is burned up, the builder will suffer loss but yet will be saved – even though only as one escaping through the flames." (1 Cor 3:12–15)

A desire for rewards motivated his service:

> "I have fought the good fight, I have finished the race, I have kept the faith. Now there is in store for me the crown of righteousness, which the Lord, the righteous Judge, will award to me on that day – and not only to me, but also to all who have longed for his appearing." (2 Tim 4:7–8)

God has not revealed how the rewards are defined or experienced and it would be unwise to speculate. What is clear is that every believer will enjoy perfect, unspoiled communion with Christ and his people (1 Thess 4:17). Thinking about this should motivate joyful and sacrificial service. We can have confidence that, in final analysis, nothing we do for Christ in this world will be wasted.

Every believer is promised a life which is full of happiness, joy and satisfaction. We will each be rewarded but since there is no sin in heaven, there can be no envy or jealousy or covetousness. Members of Christ's body will not feel cheated, inadequate or undervalued.

To seek rewards is an honourable motive for discipleship and service. We respond well to rewards and they can be good and useful as a secondary motivation for discipleship. But the more we seek to serve Christ, the more we love him and the more we find that enjoying him and his smile is more important than the reward he offers.

Imagine that I want my daughter to learn to play the piano. She is more interested in playing football. So we strike a deal. If she perseveres in her piano practice I will buy her the best football boots on the market. She puts a picture of the boots on the piano and at every practice she looks longingly at them. This goes on for six months. But over this time something strange happens. My daughter suddenly discovers how much she loves playing the piano! The more she practises the more she becomes competent and the more she enjoys her newfound skills. After a while it is difficult to judge whether she loves football more than music or vice versa.

The central attraction of heaven is not rewards. It is not freedom from pain and sin or restoration of fellowship with those we have loved and lost.

The central attraction of heaven is God himself.

CHAPTER 9

A LIFE OF SATISFACTION

Barry was converted towards the end of my time serving a church in Chippenham, Wiltshire. Years later I returned to serve a church in Bath and re-connected with him.

By this time Barry was almost at the end of his earthly life. He had a very aggressive form of cancer of the mouth which had led to the removal of most of his tongue. It had progressed so that he was no longer able to digest food or even sip water and had to be fed through a tube. I was allowed to wet his lips with water.

In spite of his dreadful condition Barry was bright and full of hope. It was difficult to make out what he was saying and it was painful for him to speak. However he was determined to tell me what gave him such confidence in the face of death. After several attempts he managed to communicate his heart:

> "They tell me that I will never be able to eat or drink again. That's okay. Soon I will be with Jesus. Soon I will be feasting with him!"

From what we have already seen feasting does not come at the moment of death but at the moment of resurrection. We can't be certain exactly what this feasting will involve, but it never crossed my mind to correct Barry's theology at this point. It was simply a matter of timing. In his central contention he was absolutely right.

Remember the words of Paul: "I desire to depart and be with Christ, which is better by far" (Phil 1:23). The central attraction and the unchanging hope of heaven is to be with Christ. Whatever joys we may experience in this life, heaven will be "better by far". This is what sustained Barry and it is what has sustained countless believers for centuries.

Either/or ...

In previous generations most of the books written about heaven emphasized the fact that the central attraction of heaven was seeing God. So, to give just one example, Jonathan Edwards writes of the "exceeding joy" that the saints have in heaven and this consists of:

> "... beholding the face of their Father, and the glory of their Redeemer, and contemplating his wonderful works, and particularly his laying down of his life for them ..."[1]

This emphasis does not deny the resurrection of the body or the reality of the new creation, but it focuses on beholding God himself and the fellowship which flows from this as the fundamental glory of heaven.

However, some recent writers question the otherworldliness often associated with this view. They are distrustful of any approach which sees the future life as one of ecstatic experience or mystical contemplation. They suggest we should pay less attention to the subjective experiences of the heart and more on our engagement with the world as it is and as it will be. For example, Richard Middleton says we must dismiss the idea that the "final destiny of the faithful is an unending worship service of perpetual praise in God's immediate presence in another world".[2]

There is much to be commended in this emphasis. The picture of heaven as a place of eternal disembodied hymn singing is an unhelpful caricature as we've already seen. We want, quite rightly, to affirm the goodness of the creation and the continuity between activities of this world and the next.

However, it seems to me that it is possible to over-react, reducing heaven to human proportions and failing to see that our one true end is communion with God. Without him all the other joys of heaven fade and dwindle. He is not only the cause of our hope he is also its centre.

In the final analysis, we do not need to make a choice between enjoying God and enjoying his gifts. In the garden of Eden, Adam both tended the garden and walked with the Lord. There was no conflict between the two.

Ray Ortlund puts it like this:

> "How big is your hope? Is the wingspan of your hope big enough to get you soaring? Is your hope big enough, imaginative enough, with wolves and lambs and lions thrown in for good measure? Hope on this grand scale – this is the gospel. It is big. It offers both the prospect of personal intimacy with God forever and a renewed world of peace and righteousness. It isn't just one or the other. God has a plan for you and for this whole world. The Lord Jesus Christ died for this, and he will not be denied."[3]

Our hope includes pain-free rest, joyful service, reunion with loved ones and the enjoyment of a new creation, all within the context of being with God himself forever.

Longing for God

I was twelve and had just become a Christian when my auntie bought me a Bible for Christmas. It was leather bound with a zip and I was so proud of it. I had a treasure worth more than gold and sweeter than honey (Psalm 19:10). I'm afraid that that particular Bible fell apart a long time ago. But I have been digging into the treasures of God's Word every day for more than fifty years. The more I discover, the more my hunger grows for more and more.

God is like that. We know him but the more we know him the more we want to know him.

This is one of the key themes of the Psalms. Consider Psalm 63 which David wrote while he was in the wilderness. He is in an arid and dangerous desert and is ringed by enemies who want to kill him. And yet his deepest longing is not for relief from trouble, but for God:

> "You, God, are my God,
> earnestly I seek you;
> I thirst for you,
> my whole being longs for you,
> in a dry and parched land
> where there is no water." (Psalm 63:1)

Trials, troubles and failures do not drive God from us. He is our God forever. His fidelity does not depend on our faithfulness. We have been loved with an everlasting love. But the affirmation soon becomes an aspiration. Knowing God ignites a desire to know him more. We have a treasure but have only just begun to plumb its depths.

In the Judean wilderness there are no streams and little shade from the relentlessness of the sun so David's thirst is overwhelming. You cannot reason with thirst. You cannot think of anything else as you yearn for water. And this is how his soul feels. He cries out for more of God. Memory of past encounters with the Lord fuels this longing:

> "I have seen you in the sanctuary
> and beheld your power and your glory." (Psalm 63:2)

He has beheld God's glory, not with a glance but with a gaze. He has seen the awesome majesty of God – not some pathetic, feeble and inconsequential god – but the glorious Creator and Covenant Lord.

And his longing to see more of this glory is not a hopeless quest. David is confident that he will once again enjoy the closeness of God's presence and the reassurance of his smile:

> "Because your love is better than life,
> my lips will glorify you.
> I will praise you as long as I live,
> and in your name I will lift up my hands.
> I will be fully satisfied as with the richest of foods;
> with singing lips my mouth will praise
> you." (Psalm 63:3–5)

His hope is based on God's covenant love; his gracious and undeserved commitment to those who have entrusted themselves to him. Our hope of heaven is based on this same unyielding love which stoops to lift unworthy people to his throne. David is confident that he will praise God with his lips and feast on him, even in the desert.

This hope causes him to cling to God (Psalm 63:7–8) and he knows that in the end all will be well:

> "But the king will rejoice in God;
> all who swear by God will glory in him,
> while the mouths of liars will be silenced." (Psalm 63:11)

Were these hopes and expectations realized during his lifetime? We do not know. What we do know is that however arid it might seem as we journey with God through this world, one day God will satisfy us with himself.

The purpose of salvation is much bigger than the forgiveness of sin. God is determined to bring us into a relationship with himself so that we can then glorify and enjoy him forever. Indeed if we want a shorthand description of the joys of heaven it is just this. We will behold our God and for eternity we will bring glory to him and enjoy him as the ongoing source of all delight.

Nothing without God

After the Israelites sinned by creating the golden calf God promises that the people will still inherit the land but goes on to declare:

> "Go up to the land flowing with milk and honey. But I will not go with you, because you are a stiff-necked people, and I might destroy you on the way." (Exod 33:3)

The people respond with lamentation:

> "When the people heard these distressing words, they began to mourn, and no one put on any ornaments." (Exod 33:4)

What is the point of having the gifts without the Giver? Without the Lord the land is an empty promise. Without

God heaven is an empty place. It is the presence of God which makes heaven into heaven.

This longing for God pulsates through the Bible and comes to its ultimate realization in heaven where "he who sits on the throne will shelter them with his presence" (Rev 7:15). This is a wonderfully intimate picture of our relationship with God. The Greek phrase literally reads "he will tabernacle over them". In the wilderness the tabernacle was the place where God met with his people. We will be brought into the safety and security of his shadow. This verse echoes the words of Ruth as she seeks the security of being married to Boaz:

> "'I am your servant Ruth,' she said. 'Spread the corner of your garment over me, since you are a guardian-redeemer of our family.'" (Ruth 3:9)

When I was courting my wife in the 1970s I used to wear a large black ex-navy duffle-coat. It would have kept me warm crossing the Atlantic in the middle of a winter storm! When Edrie felt cold I would open my coat and she would fit snugly under my arm. As I think about it I am amazed at how often she said she felt cold! This is a picture of intimacy and sanctuary and protection. God welcomes weary pilgrims into the warm embrace of his eternal love.

Listen to Samuel Rutherford:

> "O my Lord Jesus Christ, if I could be in heaven without thee, it would be hell; and if I could be in hell and have

> thee still it would be heaven to me, for thou art all the heaven that I want."[4]

Jonathan Edwards agrees:

> "God is the highest good of the reasonable creature, and the enjoyment of him is the only happiness with which our souls can be satisfied ... Fathers, mothers, husbands, wives, children or the company of earthly friends, are but shadows. But the enjoyment of God is the substance. These are but the scattered beams, but God is the sun. These are but the streams, but God is the fountain. These are but the drops, but God is the ocean."[5]

In the Bible the consummation of our heavenly delight is the vision of God and the worship which flows from this. God brings us to heaven and then invites us to enjoy him forever. Human beings were created for God and the desire to see and know and enjoy him is deeply embedded in our human nature.

Every other joy in heaven will be secondary and derived from this ultimate joy. The essence of eternal life is to know God (John 17:3).

They will see his face

The pinnacle of our delight in heaven will be the sight of God. Old Testament saints longed for this:

> "As for me, I shall be vindicated and shall see your face;
> when I awake, I shall be satisfied with seeing your likeness." (Psalm 17:15)

Jesus promised it:

> "Blessed are the pure in heart,
> for they will see God." (Matt 5:8)

And John confirms the promise:

> "They will see his face, and his name will be on their foreheads." (Rev 22:4)

The sight of God given to Moses, Paul and John were a foretaste of this, but they all recognized that their vision was limited (Exod 33:20; 1 Tim 6:16; John 1:18). In our new resurrection bodies we will be able to behold God as never before.

And I don't think that this sight of God is static. There will be infinite progress in our delight in God. The soul is like a vessel which God fills with an endless supply of his presence. We will discover more and more of the loveliness of God as he eternally communicates more and more of himself.

This suggests that in heaven we complete the journey we began on earth. As we follow Christ and drink more deeply from the wells of salvation, we will find an ever-increasing delight in God. We will never cease to wonder at his glory or the glory of heaven:

> "When we've been there ten thousand years,
> Bright shining as the sun,
> We've no less days to sing God's praise
> Than when we'd first begun."[6]

Seeing Jesus

This of course raises an important question: How can we see God "who lives in unapproachable light, whom no one has seen or can see" (1 Tim 6:16)?

The Bible teaches God's invisibility (Exod 33:20; John 1:18; 4:24; Col 1:15; 1 Tim 1:17; 6:16; 1 John 4:12). Yet it also promises that we will see him face to face. How do we understand this apparent contradiction?

The answer is that we will see Christ:

> "The seeing of God in the glorified body of Christ is the most perfect way of seeing God with the bodily eyes that can be. It is seeing a real body that one of the persons of the Trinity has assumed to be his body and that he dwells in for ever as his own and in which the divine majesty and excellency appear as much as it is possible for it to appear in outward form and shape."[7]

In the shadow of the cross the Redeemer prays that his people might be with him forever and see his glory (John 17:24). We will see the glory of God in his face (2 Cor 4:6):

> "For the Lamb at the centre of the throne
> will be their shepherd;
> 'he will lead them to springs of living water.'
> 'And God will wipe away every tear from their eyes.'" (Rev 7:17)

The Son is our Shepherd and he actively leads his people in heaven (Rev 14:4). He will continue to pastor us for eternity, as he leads his people to streams of living water.

Perhaps the only appropriate way of describing this future hope is in song:

> "The Bride eyes not her garment,
> But her dear Bridegroom's face;
> I will not gaze at glory
> But on my King of grace;
> Not at the crown He giveth
> But on His pierced hand:
> The Lamb is all the glory
> Of Immanuel's land."[8]

A world of love

Is there one characteristic of this vision of God which stands out?

For an answer we may turn to Paul's great hymn about love in 1 Corinthians 13. Having described the priority and perfections of love, Paul then speaks of its permanence. What we know of God and his love for us now is but a pale reflection of what we will know when we see him face to face:

> "For now we see only a reflection as in a mirror; then we shall see face to face. Now I know in part; then I shall know fully, even as I am fully known." (1 Cor 13:12)

And so he concludes:

> "And now these three remain: faith, hope and love. But the greatest of these is love." (1 Cor 13:13)

Faith will be rewarded with sight and hope will reach perfect fulfilment. But love will supersede both of them. God is love (1 John 4:16). He loves us more than we can imagine and he wants us to know it. Paul prayed for this for all believers in this life:

> "And I pray that you, being rooted and established in love, may have power, together with all the Lord's holy people, to grasp how wide and long and high and deep is the love of Christ, and to know this love that surpasses knowledge – that you may be filled to the measure of all the fullness of God." (Eph 3:17–19)

In heaven we will know this love in its magnificent perfection.

Jesus' arms were spread out for us on the cross. In heaven they will draw us into his eternal embrace. Richard Baxter describes it like this:

> "You will be eternally embraced in the arms of that love that is from everlasting to everlasting, of that love that brought the Son of God's love from heaven to earth, from earth to the cross, from the cross to the grave, and from the grave to glory. This is the same love that was weary, hungry, tempted, scorned, scourged, buffeted, spit upon, crucified and pierced."[9]

God is love. Before time began this love existed in profound profusion between the Father, the Son and the Holy Spirit. Because we are made in God's image we long to be loved. This longing will be totally satisfied in heaven – listen to Jonathan Edwards:

> "And in heaven, this desire of love, or this fondness of being loved, will never fail of being satisfied. No inhabitants of that blessed world will ever be grieved with the thought that they are slighted by those that they love nor that their love is not fully and fondly returned."[10]

Sometimes the trials of life seem to blot out God's love. But in heaven we will never doubt God's love. At other times our hearts feel cold and unresponsive. In heaven our hearts will burn with unquenchable love for the God who has saved us and brought us home.

More to come

Imagine a boy on his first visit to the sea. As he stands on the shore for the first time, he dips his hand in the water and exclaims: "It's wet." He then tastes it and observes: "It's salty." Finally he lifts his eyes to the horizon. "Wow! Isn't it big!"

His experience of the sea is real but incredibly limited. He knows nothing of its vastness and its undisclosed secrets. He has never been terrified by its power and unpredictability. He has never visited its subterranean mountains and volcanoes. Yes he knows something of the sea and the something he knows is true. But there is so much more to know.

When we become Christians, we are like this child. But there is more to know of God than we can ever contemplate in one short lifetime. We are overwhelmed by what we discover as each day some new vista of delight presents itself. The knowledge of God delights us but, at the same time, leaves us longing for more. We love what we find, but we are conscious that there is so much more out there to explore.

Perhaps it is true that in the whole of our lifetime we are only at the edge of discovery. Even the greatest theologians and the godliest Christians have not progressed far in the divine science of the knowledge of God. We die knowing that there is so much more of

God to know. God has set eternity in our hearts (Ecc 3:11) and we instinctively know that there is more. And surely this is the principal goal of eternal life – to grow in the knowledge of God throughout the eternal ages.

Heaven won't be dull. How could it possibly be boring to spend eternity exploring the infinite ocean of divine perfections?

PART 3

LIVING WITH HEAVEN IN VIEW

The last exam I sat was in June 1977 and I had not prepared for it.

That's slightly misleading. I didn't prepare because I couldn't. It was a three-hour unseen essay: the examiners were kind enough to give you the choice of possible titles to pick from and you were supposed to show that after three years you had become a reasonably competent theologian.

Few people like exams, but usually hard work pays off. This was different. What if you couldn't find a subject or a title that appealed to you? Three hours is a very long time to twiddle your thumbs!

When I turned over the exam paper I discovered that I didn't fancy any of the first half-dozen questions.

Then I saw it: *"The New Testament is a book of unfinished business." Discuss.*

And discuss it I did – for three hours! And I passed the exam!

The New Testament celebrates the fact that the defining moment in human history has arrived. The kingdom has come near because the King is here. But that is not the whole picture. Jesus also spoke of the kingdom in future terms, emphasizing that one day he would return to bring about the consummation of all God's promises.

The New Testament *is* a book of unfinished business.

The hope of the second coming is not an eccentric belief for people on the fringe of the faith. It is the warp and weft of the New Testament and central to all God's purposes. Jesus' return is the blessed hope of the church (Titus 2:13). And at the heart of this hope is the prospect of heaven.

But the New Testament writers are not interested in speculation about dates and timetables. Their emphasis is always on the way in which we should live our lives in the light of the future. Remember how Richard Baxter spent half an hour each day meditating on the saints' everlasting rest? In this last section we will consider three ways in which we should live with heaven in view.

CHAPTER 10

BE COMFORTED

Peter and Patricia were among the first people to make us feel welcome when I became a pastor in the beautiful city of Worcester.

To say that they were slightly eccentric is no exaggeration!

Everyone smiled when you mentioned their names – but it was always a smile of genuine affection and love. Patricia exercised the gift of hospitality to an unusual degree, befriending many who were on the fringe of Christian fellowship and making them feel welcomed and loved. Peter, a retired craft teacher, produced magnificent furniture in the Shaker style, even teaching his skills to classes in North America.

Born and bred in Yorkshire, they loved their home county and once they even arranged to take our family on holiday up to the Yorkshire Dales. We had four kids so it was quite an undertaking but they took it in their stride. And our children adored their youngest son Bruce who came with us.

They were exceptional people who were utterly self-effacing and quickly brushed aside any compliment. But what defined them was their love for Jesus. He was the centre of all that they did and they longed to know more and more of him.

And this was their great comfort when Bruce was killed in a road accident. We were at church when the news came through. They were brave, but they'd had their hearts ripped out. They carried the scars for the rest of their lives.

In later years Patricia nursed Peter through the horrors of Alzheimer's and soon after his death became seriously ill herself. Covid restrictions made visiting difficult, but because I had been her pastor I had special permission to visit her in the hospice. We talked and prayed and wept together. Both Peter and Bruce had been Christians so we talked about heaven.

Patricia asked me to read the words of Jesus in John 14:

> "Do not let your hearts be troubled. You believe in God; believe also in me. My Father's house has many rooms; if that were not so, would I have told you that I am going there to prepare a place for you? And if I go and prepare a place for you, I will come back and take you to be with me that you also may be where I am." (John 14:1–3)

When I had finished reading she smiled through her tears and said, "It is such a comfort to know that they are safe and I will soon see them. And I will see Jesus. Please will you preach on that passage at my funeral?" I promised that I would.

Patricia died a few days later.

Life is fragile

Peter and Patricia's story is like countless others that I have encountered in forty years of pastoral ministry. Suffering and pain are woven into the fabric of our lives. The reality of suffering is arguably the greatest challenge to the Christian faith. It is more than a philosophical question; we long for an explanation which gives meaning to the agony we suffer. Often suffering seems unjust and disproportionate. No matter how careful we are, sudden loss can come from a clear blue sky and we discover that the things we cherish are fragile and insubstantial.

The book of Job illustrates this perfectly.

Job woke up one morning a wealthy and prosperous man with a large and happy family. When he went to bed that night he had lost all his possessions and his children (Job 1). Later he lost his physical health and emotional well-being (Job 2–3). For the rest of the book he struggles with the relentlessness of his suffering and the unhelpful counsel of his friends.

As far as we can tell he never discovers the reason for his agony, but in rare moments of courageous faith he looks beyond his circumstances and finds hope in God:

> "I know that my redeemer lives,
> and that in the end he will stand on the earth.
> And after my skin has been destroyed,
> yet in my flesh I will see God;
> I myself will see him
> with my own eyes – I, and not another.
> How my heart yearns within me!" (Job 19:25–27)

Like Patricia and so many other Christians, Job looks beyond the pain of this world to the hope of heaven.

The glory that will be revealed in us

We could turn to many different parts of the Bible to discover this eternal perspective but let's begin with Romans 8. Paul has spent the previous chapters assuring us that through faith in Christ we now have peace with God. We have moved from condemnation to reconciliation and this results in adoption and sonship:

> "The Spirit you received does not make you slaves, so that you live in fear again; rather, the Spirit you received brought about your adoption to sonship. And by him we cry, 'Abba, Father.' The Spirit himself testifies with our spirit that we are God's children. Now if we are children, then we are heirs – heirs of God and co-heirs with Christ, if indeed we share in his sufferings in order that we may also share in his glory." (Rom 8:15–17)

God has sent his Spirit to assure us of our sonship and this means that, amazingly, we are co-heirs with Christ. What is Christ's inheritance? *Everything!* – and we are to share this inheritance.

But did you notice the sting in the tail? We will share this inheritance if we are willing to also share in his sufferings. How could it be otherwise? Jesus came to his crown through the suffering of the cross. We follow a crucified Saviour. Glory and suffering go together. The pain is the proof of the inheritance and thinking about the inheritance will help us to endure the pain.

And what we will gain will be much greater than anything we might lose:

> "I consider that our present sufferings are not worth comparing with the glory that will be revealed in us." (Rom 8:18)

Paul shares the same thought in 2 Corinthians 4:17:

> "For our light and momentary troubles are achieving for us an eternal glory that far outweighs them all."

Imagine old-fashioned kitchen scales. Ingredients are placed in one bowl and weights in the other. Into one bowl place all the sorrows and heartbreaks of this world. Think of what we suffer because we are human and the pain we feel when we lose the things we love. Add to this the scars we bear from spiritual warfare and top it up with the times we have not been able to understand God's will or when we have felt lonely and rejected. By now the bowl is full to overflowing. It certainly does not look "light and momentary"!

But now place into the other bowl a single moment in the presence of the one who has promised to wipe all tears from our eyes. Down thuds that side of the scales as "the eternal weight of glory" outweighs and outlasts all the sorrows of this life.

One thing we know

Paul continues to set our trials in the context of eternity. In the course of doing so he speaks of two great truths which "we know".

The first truth concerns the pervasiveness of suffering.

The creation struggles with the consequences of the Fall. It has been disfigured with the graffiti of sin and is therefore "subject to frustration" (Rom 8:20):

> "*We know* that the whole creation has been groaning as in the pains of childbirth right up to the present time. Not only so, but we ourselves, who have the firstfruits of the Spirit, groan inwardly as we wait eagerly for our adoption to sonship, the redemption of our bodies." (Rom 8:22–23, emphasis added)

The New Testament mentions suffering in almost every one of its twenty-seven books. But in most cases it is suffering for our faith. We suffer because we follow in the footsteps of Jesus. But these verses are concerned with the suffering we face because we are part of a fallen world. Non-Christians suffer cancer and heart disease and dementia and mental illness. And so do Christians. We are not immune because of our faith. Like the world we groan in pain and these pains are severe – like the pains of childbirth.

Anyone who tells you otherwise is misleading you.

There is no pain-free zone we can inhabit. We will not be free from suffering until we experience the "redemption of our bodies". This points forward to resurrection day.

Our trials are intensely painful but they are also immensely fruitful. And so we live in hope:

> "For in this hope we were saved. But hope that is seen is no hope at all. Who hopes for what they already have? But if we hope for what we do not yet have, we wait for it patiently." (Rom 8:24–25)

And while we groan and patiently wait for the full benefits of salvation, God has not left us on our own. He has sent the Holy Spirit to turn our groanings into prayers (Rom 8:26–27). Beneath our groaning is this sublime mystery of God the Spirit, speaking to God the Father.

Another thing we know

But there is more to help us focus on heaven. We know that we suffer, but there is something else which we know:

> "And *we know* that in all things God works for the good of those who love him, who have been called according to his purpose. For those God foreknew he also predestined to be conformed to the image of his Son, that he might be the firstborn among many brothers and sisters. And those he predestined, he also called; those he called, he also justified; those he justified, he also glorified." (Rom 8:28–30, emphasis added)

In these well-known, much-loved and often-quoted words, Paul gives us an affirmation, an explanation and a confirmation.

First the *affirmation*: life is not random.

We are not the victims of nature or fate or chance. A good and gracious Father is working deliberately and invincibly for our good. He is the Friend behind all the phenomena of our lives. And his care is comprehensive. He is not at work in some things, most things or almost all things. His control extends to everything. This includes prosperity and adversity, sickness and health, joys and sorrows, blessings and trials. God never has to wring his hands in frustration because somehow something got under his radar. He is never outmanoeuvred or taken by surprise. And this God works all things for our good. He is incapable of doing anything that is *not* good. There is always a purpose. We may not see it, but like a jigsaw, all the pieces are being fitted together to form a perfect picture.

Next the *explanation:* God's goal is to make us like Jesus.

We often struggle with some of the painful providences we experience and question how our circumstances can possibly be for our good. Let's be clear, trials are not good in and of themselves. Cancer or persecution or betrayal are not good things. I baulk at the idea that I should thank God for these things. When I see my wife suffering the ravages of multiple sclerosis am I supposed to thank God for MS? Of course not. MS is horrible. I hate it. I cannot thank God for it and I'm not being asked to do so.

What I can thank God for – what is good – is God's purpose in the trials. The trial may be vile, but the purpose is magnificent. Through our trials God is making us like Jesus and getting us ready for heaven. God is preparing "brothers and sisters" who are just like Jesus and will enjoy eternity with him. Heaven is a holy place and we are being made holy so that we will be able to enter into the full enjoyment of the heavenly realm. In our redeemed bodies freed from all pain and sin we will reign as part of Christ's family for eternal ages. Even if our present suffering seems unbearable, this heavenly perspective transforms the way in which we view it and endure it.

God is committed to making us holy and holiness means being like Jesus.

We are being transformed now as we contemplate his glory:

"And we all, who with unveiled faces contemplate the Lord's glory, are being transformed into his image with

> ever-increasing glory, which comes from the Lord, who is the Spirit." (2 Cor 3:18)

This process is never completed in this life, but will be fully accomplished when we see Christ. At that moment, "we shall be like him, for we shall see him as he is" (1 John 3:2)!

Finally the *confirmation*. God's purpose in preparing us for heaven cannot fail.

When the suffering seems brutal it is easy to lose sight of this great hope. Or perhaps we doubt our ability to survive and endure to the end. Paul anticipates these concerns and he takes his readers deep into the eternal purposes of God. Using a striking series of verbs, Paul reminds us that God's plan to make us like Jesus and then spend eternity with us, is not a last-minute response to an unforeseen crisis. God's purpose stretches from eternity to eternity.

What was God doing before he created the world? The Bible tells us that the Father loved the Son with a profound and unquenchable love. Together with the Holy Spirit the three persons of the Trinity rejoiced with perfect and eternal joy. But the Bible also tells us that the Father set his love upon us before speaking the cosmos into existence. When Paul says that God foreknew us, he's speaking of more than intellectual knowledge. He's saying that before time began God already knew and loved us. He did not see our faith ahead of time and then nudge us towards belief. He set his heart upon us. He wanted us to share the joy of heaven with him for eternity.

Because of this love, he predestined us to be conformed to the image of his Son, choosing us in Christ before the beginning of time (Eph 1:3–4). Heaven is a perfectly sinless place. How could we enjoy heaven if we were not transformed to be like Jesus? This is the purpose of predestination. Some people struggle with this doctrine but it shouldn't be a banner to march under or a truth to bomb others with. Predestination is a comfort – my hope of heaven depends not on me but on God.

Because God wanted us to share eternity with him, he called us and justified us. This has been Paul's great theme in Romans. He pardons all our sins and accepts us as righteous in his sight through the righteousness of Christ accounted to us and received by faith alone. This is more than a legal transaction. By his grace God receives sinners into his family as his very own sons and daughters.

Paul now jumps forward to glorification. This is the culmination of the process which began in eternity past. We will be raised to new life and will live with God and share in his glory forever. We will see God's face and all the sorrows of earth will flee away.

R.C. Sproul puts it like this:

> "… if we persevere through the pain and the suffering of this present world, the vision of God waits for us on the other side. Can you imagine it? Can you imagine looking into the unveiled glory of God for one second? It will make every pain I've ever experienced in this world worth it to see that … So these former things that

> cause us so much grief will pass away, and He will make all things new."[1]

Paul anticipates that his readers may consider this is too good to be true. In the following verses he assures us of the certainty of our heavenly hope. Many things may be against us, but God is for us so we are safe, even among all the uncertainties of life (Rom 8:31–32). Sometimes the memory of our sin haunts us and we fear that heaven just seems too far away. Paul reminds us that God has justified us and that Christ prays for us (Rom 8:33–34). The road to heaven is difficult and we can feel so weak and far from home. That may be true but the God who set his heart upon us in eternity, the Saviour who has gone to heaven to prepare a place for us, and the Holy Spirit who gives us a foretaste of the inheritance to come will never let us go (Eph 1:13–14).

Paul concludes:

> "For I am convinced that neither death nor life, neither angels nor demons, neither the present nor the future, nor any powers, neither height nor depth, nor anything else in all creation, will be able to separate us from the love of God that is in Christ Jesus our Lord." (Rom 8:38–39)

You are safe!

A heart of wisdom

We referred to Psalm 90 in the first chapter. Remember that it was written against the background of the death of a whole generation of men and women in the wilderness. We are mere creatures of dust and life is short and difficult, our days "quickly pass" in "trouble and sorrow" (Psalm 90:10) and so we need to think wisely about time and eternity constantly praying: "Teach us to number our days, that we may gain a heart of wisdom" (Psalm 90:12).

Imagine you have an infinitely large piece of paper in front of you. On the surface you draw a small dot. You then begin to draw a line. The line continues and continues and continues. It never stops.

The dot represents your life here and now. The line represents eternity. No matter how long we might live – seventy, eighty, ninety years or more – our days here are no more than that small dot compared with the eternity which lies before us in heaven.

Two things follow. Firstly, we must, as Moses insists, take each day as a gift from God and live it for his glory. We are to be engaged in the affairs of this world:

> "Be very careful, then, how you live – not as unwise but as wise, making the most of every opportunity, because the days are evil. Therefore do not be foolish but understand what the Lord's will is." (Eph 5:15–17)

All good things in this world come from God (James 1:17) and we are to enjoy what he sends (Ecc 2:24; 3:12–13). We are to be salt and light in the world. Thinking about heaven should not cause us to opt out and retreat into a pietistic comfort zone. We have one short life to gain treasure in heaven and so we must not waste it.

But, secondly, we should recognize just how short life is. Moses tells us to count it out in days not years. If we live to be seventy, which is not promised to any of us, we will live for around 25,567 days (depending on leap years!). That sounds a lot to me, until I realize that as I write I have already lived 24,654 days! Whatever pain we experience it will soon be over.

This is why Paul encourages "godliness with contentment" and tells us that it is "great gain" (1 Tim 6:6). We are pilgrims here and nothing in this world lasts forever. Every joy and every sorrow is temporary. We should rejoice in what we have rather than grieving over what we may have lost.

The wise pastor Richard Baxter puts it like this:

> "The frequent and believing views of glory are the most precious cordial in all afflictions: first to sustain our spirits, and make our sufferings far more easy; secondly, to stay us from repining and make us bear with patience and joy; and thirdly, to strengthen our resolutions, that we forsake not Christ for fear of trouble."[2]

Contemplating heaven will bring us comfort in the furnace of affliction.

CHAPTER 11

BE HOLY

Have you ever seen one of those ultrasound pictures that expectant parents are proud to show you?

I must have seen scores of such pictures and like many a witness I have feigned wonder and amazement at the grainy image which is so enthusiastically exhibited. But let's be honest, ultrasound photos are not very complimentary. Nonetheless we rejoice with those who rejoice, because this is a real baby – a person with potential not a potential person.

But imagine that on your first visit to see a newborn, mum stops you looking into the crib and says, "Oh don't look at baby. Look at this instead!", before proudly handing you the now much-faded ultrasound picture.

Something is seriously wrong in such a scenario. The photo served a temporary purpose, but once the real baby arrives it becomes totally redundant. There is no comparison between the shadow and the reality. Why do you want the image when you can see the real thing?

But that was what was going on in Colossae, prompting Paul to write to the church.

The apostle is in prison in Rome when he hears the disturbing news that false teachers have visited this church and are teaching that Jesus is *good* but he is *not enough*. Jesus offers a kind of secondary-school-level spirituality. They are offering something bigger and better – degree-level piety. Whether it involves new revelations or ascetic practices or mystical experiences, the added extra takes you beyond Jesus.

When Paul hears this he goes ballistic! How can they be so foolish? If you have Jesus you have everything!

> "So then, just as you received Christ Jesus as Lord, continue to live your lives in him, rooted and built up in him, strengthened in the faith as you were taught, and overflowing with thankfulness." (Col 2:6–7)

Seeking anything beyond Christ is like rejecting the baby in favour of the ultrasound picture. Jesus is the reality. In him "all the fullness of the Deity lives in bodily form" and we are "brought to fullness" (Col 2:9–10). Everything else is a shadow pointing to him:

> "Therefore do not let anyone judge you by what you eat or drink, or with regard to a religious festival, a New Moon celebration or a Sabbath day. These are a shadow of the things that were to come; the reality, however, is found in Christ." (Col 2:16–17)

How do we avoid being deceived in this way? What will protect us from being seduced by false teaching or derailed by the lure of this world? What will keep us on target?

The answer is to be heavenly minded.

Heavenly minded

Having warned the Colossian Christians of the dangers they face, Paul calls them to be heavenly minded:

> "Since, then, you have been raised with Christ, set your hearts on things above, where Christ is, seated at the right hand of God. Set your minds on things above, not on earthly things. For you died, and your life is now hidden with Christ in God. When Christ, who is your life, appears, then you also will appear with him in glory." (Col 3:1–4)

Paul has already explained they have died with Christ (Col 2:20). Now he reminds them that they have also been raised with Christ. The old life is dead and gone. Their current life is hidden with Christ in God. What is more, when Jesus returns in glory they will share that glory with him.

Paul is alluding to the breath-taking doctrine of the believer's union with Christ. By faith we have been joined to him and so we share in all his blessings and privileges. This union stretches from eternity to eternity. We were chosen "in him" before the foundation of the world (Eph 1:4,11) and we will be glorified with him in the future (Rom 8:17; 1 Cor 15:43). We remain united to Christ throughout our whole life and then for all eternity. And through this union we inherit every spiritual blessing in the heavenly realms (Eph 1:3):

> "Salvation is, in its most basic form, a participation in the Son's relationship with the Father through the power of the Holy Spirit. In our union with Christ through the Spirit, believers share in the personal relation and love between the Father and the Son, and in the manifold blessings that result."[1]

In everything Jesus did he acted as our representative. He lived for us, died for us, was raised for us, reigns for us and will return for us. In some mystical or spiritual way we have been joined to him by faith through the work of the Holy Spirit. As the bride is joined to the bridegroom (Eph 5:22–33), as the branches are joined to the vine (John 15:1–6), as the parts of the body are joined to the head (1 Cor 12:12–31), so we are joined to Christ.

This is my true identity. My whole existence is bound up with Christ. It's all about Jesus!

As I look back I remember that he left heaven to live and die for me and to purchase my salvation. He returned to heaven to present his finished work before his Father.

As I look up I see him seated at the right hand of God in heaven and I realize that that is where all my greatest treasures are because all my true treasures are found in him.

And as I look forward I am reminded that he promises to return to bring a new creation and, when he does so, I will share in his glory.

With this tender intertwining of his life with mine, it is only natural that heaven will always be forefront in my mind. When I think about Jesus I cannot help thinking of heaven. And so Paul tells his readers to "set" their hearts and minds "on things above".

Being heavenly minded is a deliberate, purposeful, continuous action on our part which involves both the affections (the heart) and the intellect (the mind). We might translate Paul's command as "be continuously seeking". It is so easy to be seduced by the things of this world – they are ever before our eyes. We have a battle on our hands – a battle for our mind and affections. The way to win the battle is to focus on Christ and heaven as we long for his return.

This is being heavenly minded.

And it will inevitably lead to a holy life now.

What on earth are you wearing?

After his call to heavenly mindedness Paul begins to show how this will affect the way in which we live now – both negatively and positively.

It is clear that both sections flow out of the call to be heavenly minded:

> "Put to death, *therefore*, whatever belongs to your earthly nature … *Therefore*, as God's chosen people,

> holy and dearly loved, clothe yourselves …" (Col 3:5,12, emphasis added)

God saved us in order to make us holy. Holiness is not an optional extra reserved for a special class of Christian converts – it is the reason God redeemed us in the first place.

God the Father chose us in Christ before the foundation of the world, so that we should be holy (Eph 1:4). God the Son shed his blood to purify a people – so that there would be a holy and pure bride (Eph 5:25–27). The agenda of God the Holy Spirit is to transform us so that we become holy (2 Cor 3:17–18). The deliberate and determined design of the triune God is to bring a holy people into existence.

To help us understand holiness, Paul uses an extended metaphor: Be careful what you wear.

When I pastored a church in Wiltshire I often had to visit local farms. They were very welcoming, but you always knew when you were near because you could smell the slurry pit which was a necessary feature of most farms.

Imagine a visitor accidentally falling into the foul-smelling pit. Once he is pulled out he discovers that his clothes are infused with the disgusting smell of raw sewage. There is no process which can make them clean. They are ruined. The poor man washes himself thoroughly and puts on new well-laundered clothes before he is ready to face the world again.

But imagine that instead of burning the ruined clothes he carefully stores them away and then one morning decides to put on these ghastly garments with their disgusting stench. It's unthinkable!

But, says Paul, that is what we do all the time.

We have been set free from the vile life we once lived and been clothed in the pure and perfect robes of righteousness which Christ has won for us. And yet we keep returning to these filthy habits and ways of life like a dog returning to its vomit (Prov 26:11; 2 Pet 2:22). Colossians 3 is a warning against such foolishness.

Instead we should put on the robes of light and beauty. Robes fit for heaven.

Put off ...

Being heavenly minded involves both "mortification" and "transformation". Transformation might sound promising but the old word "mortification" sounds rather medieval. We picture musty cells in which half-starved monks try to beat their bodies into submission. This is not what the Bible means when it uses this word.

Paul commands:

> "Put to death [or mortify, KJV], therefore, whatever belongs to your earthly nature: sexual immorality, impurity, lust, evil desires and greed, which is idolatry … You used to walk in these ways, in the life you once lived. But now you must also rid yourselves of all such things as these: anger, rage, malice, slander, and filthy language from your lips. Do not lie to each other, since you have taken off your old self with its practices and have put on

> the new self, which is being renewed in knowledge in the image of its Creator." (Col 3:5–10)

It is unmortified sin which often prevents us from thinking about heaven. Conversely, thinking about heaven should cause us to take up arms against the old nature – the way we used to think and act before we were joined to Christ by faith. We should mortify it – put it to death. As we contemplate the cost paid to purchase heaven for us, it will humble our pride and challenge us to resist sin.

We say to ourselves repeatedly: "I am going to a holy place where I will be made utterly holy forever." Dwelling on this should cause me to hate sin now and take up arms against this old nature. We are not to give it an inch. Instead we are to put it to death; strangle and stifle and starve it. We must not allow it to control us. We must not flirt with sin but flee from it. Remember the words of Jesus:

> "If your hand or your foot causes you to stumble, cut it off and throw it away. It is better for you to enter life maimed or crippled than to have two hands or two feet and be thrown into eternal fire. And if your eye causes you to stumble, gouge it out and throw it away. It is better for you to enter life with one eye than to have two eyes and be thrown into the fire of hell." (Matt 18:8–9)

That sounds pretty radical, but it's exactly what Paul is warning us about here. If we don't break sin, it will break us. If we fail to take it seriously it will ruin our lives. We cannot lose our salvation but there is a high price to pay if we live careless lives. Paul was conscious of the danger of allowing sin to disqualify him from service:

> "No, I strike a blow to my body and make it my slave so that after I have preached to others, I myself will not be disqualified for the prize." (1 Cor 9:27)

This is a reference to the self-discipline that is demanded of successful athletes. The Olympic medallist does not allow his body to control him. In matters of diet and exercise and the sacrifice of everyday pleasures he keeps his body in check.

Paul identifies two sets of sinful desires and actions which we are to resist.

The first cluster of sins involves sexual immorality. Behind all manifestations of these sins is idolatry, the worship of the self and the egotistical exploitation of others for sexual gratification. These sins provoke God's wrath because they exploit and use others as mere objects. They were common in the Colossians' pagan past and they provoked God's judgement. Their new destination is heaven and this is a holy place for holy people.

The second obnoxious cluster is associated with the way in which we respond to others. It includes anger, rage, malice, slander, filthy language and lies. Once again these are displays of the self-centredness of the "old self". When someone brushes against my self-centred ego it bristles with rage and explodes with anger or it cools down to a malevolent malice. In either case it affects the way I speak and act. Within the church all religious, ethnic and social barriers have been broken down (Col 3:11). There is no place for my sensitive ego.

A few years ago I was speaking at a conference in Buckie, Scotland. During a free afternoon a local fisherman took me out in his boat to catch some crabs. I noticed that he was very careful about the way he picked up each crab and placed it in the basket. "Of course I'm careful," he said when I commented on this. "They are fierce wee creatures. They're fresh from the sea and angry with it. I've seen a crab catch hold of a man's hand and it won't let it go. I've seen it break a man's finger rather than let go."

I wondered what you should do if you got caught, and he explained: "The only way to break its grip is smash the crab against the side of the boat. If you don't kill it, it will hurt you."

I have to be radical in the way I deal with sins.

Put on ...

But there is more to being heavenly minded than avoiding sin. Having put off the old clothes we are to put on new garments:

> "Therefore, as God's chosen people, holy and dearly loved, clothe yourselves with compassion, kindness, humility, gentleness and patience. Bear with each other and forgive one another if any of you has a grievance

> against someone. Forgive as the Lord forgave you. And over all these virtues put on love, which binds them all together in perfect unity." (Col 3:12–14)

Paul begins by reminding them of who they are. God chose you, Paul tells his readers. He changed you. He will always love you. He took the initiative to bring you into a relationship with himself. He set you aside to belong to him. He has made you holy; he is making you holy; he will make you holy. He has loved you with an everlasting love, seeing you in Christ and therefore looking on you as his dearly loved child.

These are powerful motives to cause us to want to live lives that are pleasing to him. And we do this by casting off the old filthy garments and replacing them with the beautiful new garments which Christ supplies. A new outlook demands a new outfit.

What are these new garments like? Paul mentions seven items of clothing in this wonderful wardrobe.

- *Compassion*: This involves a tenderness and a pity towards those in need. We can be full of truth but cold and clinical in the way in which we deal with each other. Instead we should sympathize with those in need and feel something of their pain.
- *Kindness*: Kindness is compassion in action. It is visible and tangible. Without it compassion is

merely sentimental. It is a deliberate desire to reach out and help others, even if it costs us to do so.

- *Humility*: We are to think more highly of others than of ourselves. The sins described earlier often stem from a fragile and over-sensitive ego. Humility is lowliness without cringing. It is a manifestation of the mind of Christ (Phil 2:5–11).
- *Gentleness*: This is associated with meekness. It is not weak or spineless. It is the opposite of a harsh, critical and judgemental spirit. My own ambitions and desires are under control so that I do not assert myself, but always seek the good of others.
- *Patience*: This could be translated "longsuffering". It means bearing with difficult people. Some people rub us up the wrong way. We are to work hard to cover their actions with a blanket of grace.
- *Forgiveness*: Where there are people there are disagreements and grievances. So how do we respond? We are to bear with each other and not keep a record of wrongs. Above all we must be willing to forgive. And we are to forgive as the Lord forgave us. That little word "as" is incredibly challenging. No matter how much we have been offended by someone else, there is no excuse for withholding forgiveness when we remember how much God has forgiven us.

- *Love*: When all the other garments are in place the last piece of clothing to put on is love. Like a belt which secures loose garments, it binds everything together. If we seek to pursue the other virtues without love our life will be distorted and unbalanced. Love is the supreme and unifying virtue. Love is many faceted but at its heart it is the willingness to act for the good of others no matter how much it costs me.

These are the garments that pilgrims wear on the journey to heaven.

And these virtues are most perfectly seen in the life of Jesus who dealt with people in compassion and mercy; who humbled himself, stooping to die on the cross; who was gentle and lowly in heart; who prayed for the forgiveness of his enemies; who is the supreme example of love as he gave himself up to be an atoning sacrifice. This is what he was on earth and this is what he is in heaven. And we will be like him!

So thinking about heaven and contemplating the glory of our Redeemer should make us hate sin and long for holiness now. We should be more concerned about how we dress our souls than how we dress our bodies. As we get up each morning and face the day, we should always and deliberately "put on" these garments.

Did you get dressed for heaven this morning?

CHAPTER 12

BE STEADFAST

Eric Liddell won the gold medal in the 400 metres at the 1924 Paris Olympics.

Eric specialized in the 100 and 200 metres sprint but refused to run in one of the 100 metre heats since it was on a Sunday. As a compromise he was entered for the 400 metres instead. No one expected him to win but he not only came in first, he set a new world record with a time of 47.6 seconds. When asked about his winning strategy, Liddell was reported to have answered:

> "The secret to my success over the 400m is that I run the first 200m as hard as I can. Then, for the second 200m, with God's help, I run harder."[1]

This is a great metaphor for the Christian life.

We might have had a good start but we can't ease off the pace as time goes on. The closer we get, the harder we should run! The journey to heaven is a lifelong commitment to following Jesus Christ. And it's not easy. We follow a Saviour who reached his crown by way of the cross.

Jesus was very clear about the cost of discipleship:

> "Then Jesus said to his disciples, 'Whoever wants to be my disciple must deny themselves and take up their cross and follow me.'" (Matt 16:24)

Jesus is not addressing the elite of the elect. This is normal Christianity – Discipleship 101! A man carrying a cross is a dead man walking. And this is how Jesus describes the route both he and we must take.

But he looks beyond the cross to the crown:

> "For whoever wants to save their life will lose it, but whoever loses their life for me will find it. What good will it be for someone to gain the whole world, yet forfeit their soul? Or what can anyone give in exchange for their soul? For the Son of Man is going to come in his Father's glory with his angels, and then he will reward each person according to what they have done." (Matt 16:25–27)

And those who follow in his footsteps will find their lives even if they have to lose them first. They will receive their reward. Nearer to Jerusalem, Jesus makes this even more clear:

> "And everyone who has left houses or brothers or sisters or father or mother or wife or children or fields for

> my sake will receive a hundred times as much and will inherit eternal life." (Matt 19:29)

So the call is to persevere on the road to heaven. The Christian life is a long obedience in the same direction.

"For me to live …"

Paul picks up this theme when he writes to the Christians in Philippi. He is under house arrest in Rome awaiting trial before Nero. Although his future looked very uncertain, his letter is marked out by an overwhelming sense of joy and confidence. However although the letter throbs with joy, this is not its supreme focus. What dominates Paul's thinking is Jesus Christ. In 104 verses Jesus is mentioned in one way or another over 50 times.

Christ dominates Paul's horizon.

Here is Paul's personal philosophy of life: "For to me, to live is Christ …" (Phil 1:21). I love him and live for him and long for him. I praise him as my Saviour and adore him as my God. I follow him as my Master and trust him as my older Brother. I preach him and serve him and am utterly satisfied with him. So when people strip me of present comforts and earthly pleasures I find my joy in him.

And if "to live is Christ" is true, then "… to die is gain" (Phil 1:21). To depart from this life is, for the apostle, to enter into the presence of Christ.

How does this affect his present thinking as he faces the uncertainties of a Roman trial?

> "If I am to go on living in the body, this will mean fruitful labour for me. Yet what shall I choose? I do not know! I am torn between the two: I desire to depart and be with Christ, which is better by far; but it is more necessary for you that I remain in the body." (Phil 1:22–24)

If you push me, says Paul, I am not afraid to die, in fact I am looking forward to it. The only thing that holds me back is my love for you. I want to serve you, and to do that it's necessary I stay in the body.

The word "depart" suggests a journey. But it is not a journey into the unknown.

Imagine a Centurion stationed on the edge of the Empire, perhaps on the wild northern frontier of Britannia guarding Hadrian's wall. It is cold and wet and barren and dangerous. He dreams of home – his little farm in Calabria where his wife and family are waiting for him. At home the sun always shines and the grapes are succulent and rebellious tribesmen are miles away beyond the borders of the Empire. One day the news arrives. His time of service is completed. The Empire is grateful for his sacrifice and is about to put a small fortune in his pocket and send him home. The time has come for his departure.

How does he feel? Overjoyed. Ecstatic. He cannot wait.

This is how Paul felt about his departure. Yes he will be temporarily away from the body, but he will be at home with the Lord. He yearns to depart.

Following Paul's example

The certainty of resurrection and the joy of the new creation drives Paul onwards and is the foundation of his hope. However he knows that he still has some way to go and this hope encourages him to persevere (Phil 3:7–9).

In Philippians 3:12–21 Paul returns to the metaphor of the athlete competing in a gruelling race. There are three exhortations as we keep our eyes on the horizon and long for heaven.

Paul begins his call to press on with an honest confession:

> "Not that I have already obtained all this, or have already arrived at my goal … Brothers and sisters, I do not consider myself yet to have taken hold of it." (Phil 3:12–13)

Paul is on his way to glory where he'll be free from the sickening presence of sin and failure. There will be no battle with depression or disease or death for any of us in heaven. But we are not there yet!

In heaven we will have an unclouded view of Christ and our hearts will never long after other things. We will be filled with joy as we gaze on our Redeemer and we will never again drift from our first love. We will no longer be prone to wander. But we are not there yet!

In heaven the spiritual battle will be over. Satan will be subdued and will never attack us again. We will find rest in the presence of the Captain of our salvation who has subdued all his foes. But we are not there yet!

Sometimes the road is rough and steep and we are tempted to give up. Hiding our doubts and fears and failures is unhelpful. Honestly confessing our need puts us in the place where we can draw on his strength, a strength which is made perfect in our weakness.

And Paul's honesty does not lead to despair. Instead he humbly commits himself to courageous perseverance:

> "I press on to take hold of that for which Christ Jesus took hold of me … Forgetting what is behind and straining toward what is ahead, I press on …" (Phil 3:12–14)

Paul is determined to gain the heavenly prize. He is therefore single-minded and wholehearted in his commitment. He refuses to dwell on the past. Neither gloomy days of failure nor glory days of victory will hold him back. Instead he fixes his eyes on the prize. The word for prize refers to the laurel crown given to victorious athletes. It was sometimes placed on a pole next to the finishing line so that the runner could see it as he rounded the last bend. This is what spurred Paul on. He could see the prize before him and it gave him a fresh determination and new zeal to press on.

There are no easy steps to Christian perfection and no shortcuts to heaven. We are a work in progress. One mark of maturity is that we hold on to what we have and continue to endure (Phil 3:15–16). We just have to keep going fixing our eyes on the prize. And of course the prize is Christ himself. So we keep our eyes fixed on him.

Press on!

Watch out

Every year the city of Bath holds a half marathon. Standing in the crowd one year I noticed a young lady who seemed to know every runner personally. As they passed she cheered them on using their personal names: "Come on Bill ... Mary ... Jo ... you're almost there!"

I was amazed at how many people she knew, until it dawned on me that she was just reading the names off their vests! Nonetheless the personal word of encouragement spurred them on and I noticed how well they responded.

The journey to heaven is a lifelong race and takes all we have got. We need to encourage each other. The company we keep will determine how effective we are in running the race set before us.

If we want to complete the race we need to keep our eyes on those who have run before us and keep in step with them. Think of the "great cloud of witnesses" described in Hebrews, who desired a "heavenly country" and lived their lives looking forward (Heb 12:1; 11:16).

But there are bad examples to avoid as well as good examples to follow. Paul tells the Philippians to "Watch out for those dogs, those evildoers, those mutilators of the flesh" (Phil 3:2). He calls them dogs. Don't think of the fluffy family pet; think rather of vile, vicious, disease-infested wild dogs. One bite will poison you. False teaching is as dangerous as that.

He now describes another group of false teachers who are "enemies of the cross" (Phil 3:18–19). They are marked out by three things.

Firstly, "their god is their stomach". This does not necessarily mean that they are gluttons. Rather they are driven by their appetites – lust, greed, envy, pride, self-interest. Their behaviour is dictated by "if it feels good do it" morality. How can a thing be bad if it feels so good?

Secondly, "their glory is in their shame". They have moved beyond self-evident standards of right and wrong. Searing their consciences they no longer feel the sting of guilt or shame. Their ethics are elastic, accommodating whatever pleases them. Instead of shame, they are proud of their sin. They have moved from hiding their wrongdoing, to excusing it, to boasting about it. There is no reasoning with people who say good is evil and evil is good.

Thirdly, "their mind is set on earthly things". This is the fatal flaw and the root of everything else. They have no conception of heaven and hell. They see the present life as the only reality. If there is no resurrection and no judgement and this is all there is, then why not live as you please? But of course they are wrong, Christ has risen and their end is destruction.

Why does Paul give this warning? Because we are surrounded by people who share the belief system of these false teachers. And it is easy to be infected. The lure of sin and the prevailing attitude of the heaven-denying culture may cause eternity to fade from the front of our minds.

Watch out!

Look up

Philippi was a Roman city in the midst of Greece. Many of the inhabitants were retired Roman soldiers. Even though they were a long way from home they maintained strong ties with Rome. Think of expatriate enclaves on the Costa-del-Sol where you can buy British newspapers, eat fish and chips and drink in an English-style pub. That was Philippi. They spoke Latin, dressed and ate and celebrated like Romans. All their laws, customs and entertainments were Roman. They were a mini Rome away from Rome.

Likewise Christians have strong ties to glory; their loyalty is there:

> "But our citizenship is in heaven. And we eagerly await a Saviour from there, the Lord Jesus Christ, who, by the power that enables him to bring everything under his control, will transform our lowly bodies so that they will be like his glorious body." (Phil 3:20–21)

Surrounded by a culture which is always alien, focused as it is on earthly things, we are citizens of heaven. This world is the bridge over which we pass to reach our ultimate destination, our true destiny. We may spend a long time on the bridge, but it would be fatal to settle there. Our Father and our Saviour, our brothers and sisters, our treasure and our inheritance, our rewards and our rest, are all on the other side of the bridge.

We are eagerly awaiting three things.

Firstly, we are longing for the return of Christ, the Saviour who will come from heaven. The return of Christ is one of the great themes of the New Testament. Jesus commanded his disciples to be ready because no one would know the date in advance (Matt 24:36,44). Angels assured the disciples Jesus would return in the same way that he had left (Acts 1:10–11).

Christians are those who "wait for [God's] Son from heaven, whom he raised from the dead – Jesus, who rescues us from the coming wrath" (1 Thess 1:10). In the last chapter of the Bible there are three occasions when Jesus assures us of his return, culminating in the final promise and the final prayer in the Bible:

> "He who testifies to these things says, 'Yes,
> I am coming soon.'
> Amen. Come, Lord Jesus.
> The grace of the Lord Jesus be with God's people.
> Amen." (Rev 22:20–21)

We are looking for Jesus. He is the only prize worth securing. He is the treasure, which is so valuable that we should be willing to sacrifice anything to gain him. What keeps me going? What helps me to persevere? What keeps me fresh and vibrant to the end? It is the prospect of being with Christ forever in that place where faith gives way to sight, where hope receives its final reward and where love remains forever satisfied with the object of its devotion.

Secondly, we are waiting for the day when this Saviour will "bring everything under his control". When he returns, history will have reached its climax and he will bring everything under his dominion:

> "With all wisdom and understanding, he made known to us the mystery of his will according to his good pleasure, which he purposed in Christ, to be put into effect when the times reach their fulfilment – to bring unity to all things in heaven and on earth under Christ." (Eph 1:8–10)

A world currently fractured and broken will be restored to pristine beauty and glory. Remember how Jesus once fell asleep in the middle of a storm which threatened to capsize the boat and kill his disciples? Once awoken, Mark tells us:

> "He got up, rebuked the wind and said to the waves, 'Quiet! Be still!' Then the wind died down and it was completely calm." (Mark 4:39)

Chaos becomes order; peril becomes peace; turmoil becomes calm. What Jesus did on the lake that day will be repeated in the whole cosmos. There is a new heaven and earth coming in which righteousness dwells.

Finally, we are longing for the moment when he "will transform our lowly bodies so that they will be like his glorious body". Our present bodies are weak and transient. They really are lowly. If we do not feel it when we are young, old age will become our educator (Ecc 12:1–5). Someone has described later years as the metallic age when you have gold in your teeth, silver in your hair and lead in your boots! But there is a better time coming:

> "Listen, I tell you a mystery: we will not all sleep, but we will all be changed – in a flash, in the twinkling of an eye, at the last trumpet. For the trumpet will sound, the dead will be raised imperishable, and we will be changed. For the perishable must clothe itself with the imperishable, and the mortal with immortality. When the perishable has been clothed with the imperishable, and the mortal with immortality, then the saying that is written will come true: 'Death has been swallowed up in victory.'" (1 Cor 15:51–54)

Our experience here is transitory. In whatever colours we paint our hope, heaven will prove to be more intense than anything we have ever imagined. It will include the full enjoyment of all the wholesome earthly pleasures we currently experience in part, just as in Eden, Adam had perfect health and relationships and a mandate to serve as God's vice-regent on earth.

Yet the greatest blessing of Eden was the proximity of Adam to his God. But Christ re-gained it. He grants the saints *more* than Adam lost. Our relationship with the Father is restored in Christ and fully realized in heaven.

So whether we are gathering around the throne to join with the angels in the worship, or serving God as we explore and enjoy the new creation, it is his presence that makes heaven the place that it is.

The anticipation of all these delights gives us the ability to endure and remain steadfast whatever we have to face.

Look up!

CONCLUSION

My dad was a big bloke.

He was a massive part of my life and then suddenly he was gone. I can't say that I think about him every day, but there are times when something will remind me of his wicked sense of humour or his gentleness and generosity.

Dad was paid on a Friday afternoon. I don't think my dad ever had a bank account and as a child I remember lying on my parents' bed and watching as he put small amounts of money from his wage packet into various boxes which he kept on top of his wardrobe. There was a box for bills and a box for Christmas and a box for our annual holiday in Blackpool.

Sorting through the garage a couple of years ago, I found one of dad's savings boxes and a wave of nostalgic love flooded over me. Memories can catch you unawares when you least expect them.

I owe so much to my dad and one of the things for which I will always be grateful is that he got me thinking about heaven. When he died, I wanted to know where he was and I wanted to know whether we would meet again in the future. Where would we spend eternity? What would it be like? I wanted to develop the habit of "looking upwards all day" like the godly minister of a previous generation Robert Murray M'Cheyne.[1]

After more than thirty years of careful inquiry I know a little more than I did on that sad day when my dad departed to be with Christ. There is still so much that I still do not know but the things of which I am certain have changed my life.

Thinking about heaven – seeking to glimpse glory – is more than an academic theological exercise. It enables us to live and die well. The best is yet to be! In the words of Timothy Keller:

> "But resurrection is not just consolation – it is restoration. We get it all back – the love, the loved ones, the goods, the beauties of this life – but in new, unimaginable degrees of glory and joy and strength."[2]

So with confidence and courage run the race with your eyes on the goal.

Or as the writer to the Hebrews puts it:

> "Therefore, since we are surrounded by such a great cloud of witnesses, let us throw off everything that hinders and the sin that so easily entangles. And let us run with perseverance the race marked out for us, fixing our eyes on Jesus, the pioneer and perfecter of faith. For

the joy set before him he endured the cross, scorning its shame, and sat down at the right hand of the throne of God." (Heb 12:1–2)

ACKNOWLEDGMENTS

I would like to thank Marjie Hutchison, Hilary Jackson, Howard Jackson, Bill James, Don Morrison, Andy Mountford and Mostyn Roberts.

Thank you for your help in preparing this book. Thank you for reading the manuscript and for your wise, insightful comments.

DISCUSSION QUESTIONS

Chapter 1: Where Is Your Heart?

1. Read Matthew 6:19–21. What do you think Jesus means when he talks about treasure in heaven? How should this affect the way we live now? What difference would it make to your life if you spent half an hour a day thinking about heaven?
2. Do you think that it is true that "we no longer think or talk or prepare for heaven as much as people of previous generations"? Why?
3. Read Hebrews 11:8–10 and 11:13–16. What do these verses teach about living with the end in view?

Chapter 2: Where Is Your Hope?

1. "Life is difficult ... The only qualification for suffering is to live long enough. No one is immune." Is this true? How does hope help?

2. Jesus is the hope of the world – indeed the only hope of the world – and Christians are his vehicle for expressing this hope. How do we express this hope as individual Christians and as the church?

3. "Death is still an enemy, but it is no longer the ogre it once was." How should we, as Christians, think about death?

4. Peter speaks of our hope in terms of an inheritance. What does this suggest? What do the following verses tell us about this inheritance? Galatians 3:18; Ephesians 1:14, 5:5; Colossians 3:24; Hebrews 9:15.

Chapter 3: What's the Big Picture?

1. Why do Christians struggle with the book of Revelation? How should the fact that it is God's picture book written to encourage struggling Christians help us to interpret it?

2. At the moment we live in "the middle of the book". We are no longer in Eden and we are not yet in heaven. How should this affect the way we respond to pain and suffering now?

3. Read Genesis 1–3 and Revelation 21:1–22:6. What parallels do you find between the two passages? What is the same and what is different?

4. What strikes you most about the picture of heaven in the final vision? How should it affect the way in which we live today?

Chapter 4: What About ...?

1. Read Revelation 4–5. What does it teach us about heaven as it exists at this moment in time?
2. Think about what the Bible tells us about the period between our death and resurrection. How is it better than our current existence? How is it inferior to our final state?
3. Are you persuaded that the Bible promises the restoration of the earth rather than its liquidation? If this is true, what are the implications for how we live in the present?
4. Accepting that our ultimate destiny is here, in a renewed earth, what do you think will be different and what will be the same?

Chapter 5: A Bodily Life

1. Why do you think that people say that they wouldn't want to go to heaven because it sounds boring? How would you answer them?
2. Why might someone say: "The most important part of me is my soul – it's far more important than my body"? Would they be right? What does 1 Timothy 4:1–5 teach on this subject?

3. The resurrection of Jesus Christ really happened and it is really important. What is the evidence that it happened? Why is it really important?

4. Read 1 Corinthians 15:53–58. Why does Paul erupt with praise in verse 57? What instructions does he give in verse 58?

Chapter 6: A Social Life

1. "A popular concept of heaven is of solitary communion between the soul and God." Why do people think like this? What is wrong with this view?

2. What do you enjoy most about being with other Christians now? How do you think that this will be magnified in heaven?

3. In heaven there are many meetings and lots of stories of grace to tell. Why will this be a great joy?

4. Paul tells us that he carried a burden for people who were not saved (Romans 9:1–3). We all know we should be burdened for the lost like Paul, but often lack his passion. What should we do about this and how can we avoid being overwhelmed?

Chapter 7: A Life of Rest

1. In what ways do we experience a lack of rest in this world?

2. Look again at Jesus' words in Matthew 11:28–30. What does Jesus say about himself? How does this encourage us to come to him? What does he mean when he says that his burden is light?

3. The devil is compared to a dragon and a lion and sometimes he appears as an angel of light. How do these images help us to understand his nature and his tactics?

4. Do you agree that the greatest battle we have to face in this life is the battle against sin? How does the hope of rest from this battle help us to resist sin now?

Chapter 8: A Life of Activity

1. "Worship is the total response of all I am to all that God has revealed of himself to me." How does Psalm 100 illustrate this?

2. Look at the five songs recorded in Revelation 4–5. What do they teach us about God? What do they teach us about worship?

3. Rest is not the cessation of activities, but the experience of reaching a goal that is crucially important to us. What goals might we reach in heaven which we have failed to reach on earth?

4. Someone might argue that: "Thinking about rewards in heaven means that we serve God for the wrong motives." How do we avoid being

mercenary? How can the idea of rewards help us to endure?

Chapter 9: A Life of Satisfaction

1. Read Psalm 42. What does the psalm reveal about the yearnings of the psalmist? How does he encourage himself? How could we use this Psalm to sharpen our longings for heaven?
2. It is often a temptation to enjoy all the gifts that God has given to us and to forget the Giver of those gifts. Why do we do this? How do we avoid doing it?
3. "O my Lord Jesus Christ, if I could be in heaven without thee, it would be hell; and if I could be in hell and have thee still it would be heaven to me, for thou art all the heaven that I want." What does this teach us about the nature of heaven and the way we should prepare for it?
4. Read Revelation 1:9–18. This describes John's vison of Jesus. What do we learn from the symbols? How does John respond and what does Jesus do?

Chapter 10: Be Comforted

1. How would you answer someone who told you that if you had more faith you would not suffer?
2. Paul assures his readers that God's purpose in preparing them for heaven cannot fail

(Rom 8:28–30). What questions does he anticipate in Romans 8:31–39? How does he answer these questions?

3. What perspective on suffering does Jesus give us in Luke 13:1–5? What questions should it raise in our minds?
4. What practical lessons can you glean from this chapter?

Chapter 11: Be Holy

1. In what ways do we fail to trust that Jesus is sufficient and try adding to him? What are the "Jesus-plus" temptations we fall into? (Hint: it might be a doctrine or an experience or a practice.)
2. Read through the list of sins described in Col 3:5–11. How do they manifest themselves in our personal lives and within the church? What are our motives for putting these things to death?
3. "Therefore, as God's chosen people, holy and dearly loved, clothe yourselves …" How does Paul describe Christians?
4. Read through the list of seven garments Paul encourages us to wear. Are you wearing all these garments at the moment? Which areas do you need to address?

Chapter 12: Be Steadfast

1. "A man carrying a cross is a dead man walking." For some Christians their faith has resulted in physical persecution and even death. What crosses do we have to bear?
2. Who inspires your faith? Read through Hebrews 11. How can their faith help us?
3. "The lure of sin and the prevailing attitude of the heaven-denying culture may cause eternity to fade from the front of our minds." How do we resist this?
4. The New Testament throbs with the promise of the return of Christ. What passages do you know which speak of this? If it is so important why do we neglect it?

SCRIPTURE INDEX

2 Chronicles

Job

Psalms

Proverbs

Ecclesiastes

Isaiah

Ezekiel

Daniel

Micah

Matthew

Mark

Luke

John

Acts

Romans

1 Corinthians

2 Corinthians

Galatians

Ephesians

Philippians

Colossians

1 Thessalonians

GENERAL INDEX

N

O

P

R

S

ENDNOTES

Chapter 1: Where Is Your Heart?

1 Richard Baxter & Tim Cooper, *The Saints' Everlasting Rest: Updated and Abridged* (Crossway, 2022), p. 137.

2 C.S. Lewis, *Mere Christianity* (Harper San Francisco, 2001), pp. 134–135.

Chapter 2: Where Is Your Hope?

1 "Florence Chadwick 1953–1964," Queen of the Channel (Channel Swimming Association, Ltd.), <https://www.queenofthechannel.com/florence-chadwick> [accessed 24/09/24].

2 Dante Alighieri, *The Divine Comedy*, trans. by Allen Mandelbaum (Everyman, 1995), p. 68.

3 Timothy Keller, *The Meaning of Marriage: Facing the Complexities of Marriage with the Wisdom of God* (Hodder & Stoughton, 2013), p. 44.

4 Priscilla Jane Owen, "We Have an Anchor", (1882).

Chapter 3: What's the Big Picture?

1 John Newton, "Glorious Things of Thee are Spoken", (1779).

2 John Henry Newman (1801–1890), "Support Us All the Day Long", A Collection of Prayers, <https://acollectionofprayers.com/2016/06/23/support-us-all-the-day-long/> [accessed 25/10/2024].

Chapter 4: What About ...?

1 Wilbur M. Smith, *The Biblical Doctrine of Heaven* (Moody Press, 1968), pp. 27–76.

2 Paul A. Marshall, *Heaven Is Not My Home: Learning to Live in God's Creation* (Word Pub, 1998), pp. 247, 249.

3 Robert L. Dabney, *Lectures in Systematic Theology* (Zondervan Reprint Edition, 1972), p. 852.

Chapter 5: A Bodily Life

1 George Bernard Shaw, *A Treatise on Parents and Children* (1920), (OTB eBook Publishing, 24 Nov 2022).

2 Richard Dawkins quoted in Joshua St. Clare, "Richard Dawkins Tells Joe Rogan Why He Thinks Heaven Would Be 'Unbelievably Boring'", *Men's Health*, 22 Oct 2019, <https://www.menshealth.com/entertainment/a29549482/joe-rogan-experience-richard-dawkins-god/> [accessed 24/09/2024].

3 John Piper, *Future Grace* (Multnomah Press, 1995), pp. 394–395.

4 Michael Horton, *The Christian Faith: A Systematic Theology for Pilgrims* (Zondervan, 2011), p. 916.

5 Joni Eareckson Tada, *Heaven: Your Real Home* (Zondervan, 1995), p. 53.

6 Robert Letham, *Systematic Theology* (Crossway, 2019), p. 865.

7 Timothy Keller, *Walking with God through Pain and Suffering* (Hodder & Stoughton, 2013), p. 59.

Chapter 6: A Social Life

1 John M. Frame, *Systematic Theology: An Introduction to the Christian Faith* (P&R Publishing, 2013), p. 1079.

2 J.I. Packer, "Hell's Final Enigma", *Christianity Today*, 22 April 2002, p. 84.

Chapter 7: A Life of Rest

1 "Baxter to an unnamed friend, February 1647" in Don Gilbert, *Undeserved Mercies: The Life of Richard Baxter (1615–1691)* (Don Gilbert, 2016), p. 171.

2 Richard Baxter & Tim Cooper, *The Saints' Everlasting Rest: Updated and Abridged* (Crossway, 2022), p. v.

3 Ibid., p. 27.

4 Ibid., p. 35.

5 Ibid., p. 35.

6 Paul Helm, *The Last Things: Death, Judgment, Heaven, and Hell* (Banner of Truth, 1989), p. 92.

7 Edward Donnelly, *Heaven and Hell* (Banner of Truth, 2001), p. 99.

8 John Bunyan, *The Pilgrim's Progress* (Wordsworth edition, 1996), p. 210.

Chapter 8: A Life of Activity

1 Donald Macleod, *A Faith to Live By: Understanding Christian Doctrine* (Christian Focus Publications, 2016), p. 308.

2 Wilbur M. Smith, *The Biblical Doctrine of Heaven* (Moody Press, 1968), p. 195.

3 Bruce Milne, *The Message of Heaven and Hell, The Bible Speaks Today* (IVP, 2002), pp. 321–322.

4 Arthur O. Roberts, *Exploring Heaven: What Great Christian Thinkers Tell Us About Our Afterlife With God* (Harper San Francisco, 2003), p. 148.

Chapter 9: A Life of Satisfaction

1 Jonathan Edwards, *Religious Affections in The Works of Jonathan Edwards, Vol 2* (Yale University Press, 1969), p. 114.

2 J. Richard Middleton, *A New Heaven and a New Earth: Reclaiming Biblical Eschatology* (Baker Academic, 2014), p. 23.

3 Raymond C. Ortlund Jr., *Isaiah: God Saves Sinners, Preaching the Word* (Crossway, 2005), p. 445.

4 Samuel Rutherford quoted in Charles H. Spurgeon, "January 17, morning", *Morning and Evening* (Aneko Press, 2001).

5 Jonathan Edwards quoted in Alister E. McGrath, *A Brief History of Heaven* (Blackwell, 2003), p. 115.

6 John Newton, "Amazing Grace", (1779).

7 Jonathan Edwards quoted in John H. Gerstner, *Jonathan Edwards on Heaven and Hell* (Baker, 1980), p. 317.

8 Anne Cousins, "The Sands of Time are Sinking", (1857).

9 Richard Baxter & Tim Cooper, *The Saints' Everlasting Rest: Updated and Abridged* (Crossway, 2022), p. 39.

10 Jonathan Edwards, *Heaven Is a World of Love* (Crossway, 2020), p. 57.

Chapter 10: Be Comforted

1 R.C. Sproul, "When All Things Are Made New", Ligonier Ministries, 1 July 2017, <https://www.ligonier.org/learn/articles/when-all-things-are-made-new> [accessed 27/09/2024].

2 Richard Baxter & Tim Cooper, *The Saints' Everlasting Rest: Updated and Abridged* (Crossway, 2022), p. 115.

Chapter 11: Be Holy

1 Marcus Peter Johnson, *One with Christ: An Evangelical Theology of Salvation* (Crossway, 2013), p. 21.

Chapter 12: Be Steadfast

1 F.A.M. Webster quoted in John W. Keddie, *Running the Race: Eric Liddell Olympic Champion and Missionary* (Evangelical Press, 2007), p. 117.

Conclusion

1 Andrew Bonar, *Memoir and Remains of Robert Murray M'Cheyne* (Banner of Truth, 1996), p. 64.

2 Timothy Keller, *Walking with God through Pain and Suffering* (Hodder & Stoughton, 2013), p. 59.